The Candy Horse
(Life As She Sees It)

by
Dorothy J. Hamilton

ISBN 0-7596-9663-2

This book is printed on acid free paper.

1stBooks – rev. 03/19/02

Dedicated to Helen Sinclair of Sinclair Arabians for breeding Stick O'Candy and selling her to us. Also dedicated to Dorothy Jane Saunders Hamilton for telling Candy's story. And finally, dedicated to Gail Trickey of Wind Drinker Arabians for making this book come to life.

Table of Contents

Introduction to Stick O'Candy's Family

"Nine houses later and an estate of $1.76" is how Robert Hamilton describes our life with Stick O'Candy and her fellow Arabians. It began some fifty years ago and continues on to this day - here I'll tell it in Bob's own words.

Robert Ward Hamilton

"It all started when my Father, Janie's grandfather, rode up into the front yard of my nice home in the north part of Mason City, Iowa on his horse, Major and put her (Janie) up in front of him on his saddle when she was around 4 1/2 years old and took her riding with him--from then on she rode everything from the kitchen chairs to the banisters pretending they were horses!!! One day when she was about 11 years old, I came home at lunch-time to learn that she and her mother Dorothy Jane had bought their first horse "Sir Robert" an American Saddlebred gelding (even though to this day they contend I, Robert Ward Hamilton, bought him. For the next two years we went through an assortment of "Sale Barn horses" safe while they were skinny but dangerous when they had weight on and we made our first move to the "country"-a half acre house next to the Mason City Country Club which Dorothy Jane soon named "El Rancho Teeny Weeny".

You have to know my family's background to understand what a big change in the style of living this adventure with horses would create.

Senior Hamilton and Bob

"Dinpop" alias Ward R. Hamilton, my grandfather was a noted north Iowa schoolman/educator - he founded Hamilton College of Commerce in 1904. He and my father, Robert W. Hamilton, later renamed it Hamilton Business College located in Mason City, Iowa

- it is still in existence. Dinpop filled my ears about when he was a young man and his various adventures with horses. Oh how I dreamed of having a horse! He also took me horseback riding with him which just added fuel to the fire.

Dorothy Jane Hamilton in dance costume.

That man whose name is "Mister" - Robert Ward Hamilton - that's who really started this grand adventure of ours, or maybe it was the business college that started this for us. You see each Fall, Spring and Summer when new quarters started at the College - he had to do his share of visiting young people in the surrounding communities telling them the advantages of having advanced training. The Sinclair Arabian Horse Farm was located in the small town of Hayward, Minnesota. Bob was driving through this small town where he saw this absolutely glorious grey horse gracefully running through his field - he was sheer beauty and he had to stop to see him - Bob met Chet and Helen Sinclair and was introduced to Gabbar, a son of Fay-el-Dine and Bride Rose. Bob returned to visit their farm and brought my mother and me to see these beautiful, gentle, wonderful Arabian horses! Bob then realized that he had always wanted an Arabian horse and by then we all three were in love with these particular Arabians. We made many, many visits north to see them. They had two fillies for sale; one a part-Arabian who was Gabbar's first foal named "Stick O'Candy" and the other was a purebred filly named Gal Azal (her nickname was "Lady Bug"). They had the same price on both fillies - both were chestnut, but Candy was something special. We made a decision to purchase Stick O'Candy but first we had to get her new home ready for her before she could come home to us. And we had to learn how to take care of a little horse, since this would be a whole new experience for us. We wanted to make sure everything would be just right for her.

Dorothy is third from the left.

Did I say we were city people. We were! We had all lived in the city prior to this new life we were to undertake. Bob was a humble accounting teacher who rose up through the ranks to become president of Hamilton Business College and just because his family owned it - as he is prone to say - didn't have anything to do with it.

"The Lady" - my mother, Dorothy Jane Saunders Hamilton, had been a professional ballet dancer who owned and operated a dance studio in Mason City, Iowa. After she had danced professionally in road shows by Eddie Foy, Jr., Eddie Cantor, Jay C. Flippen, and in Cab Calloway's "Strike Me Pink" production. She was also a business school teacher in the family owned College. Plus she also wrote continuity for the KGLO Channel 13 television station in Mason City, Iowa. She was a breeder of fine, purebred Arabian show horses through the families nationally known Candyhorse Farm in Rockford, Iowa and now in Grand Ridge, Florida.

Jane Hamilton at 12 years of age (aka Honey).

The Lady wrote Candy's story with love and a great deal of patience. Through her acquaintance with the renowned Arabian authority, Gladys Brown Edwards, she was able to have Ms. Edwards critique Candy's story.

"Honey", well that's me, Jane Marie Hamilton, and I had the very great privilege of being Candy's companion and partner.

Here then, is Stick O'Candy's story...

GLADYS BROWN EDWARDS
11341 Norwood Ave.
La Sierra, California

13 May 64

Dear Mrs. Hamilton:

Many thanks for allowing me to read "The Candy Horse". Needless to say I enjoyed it very much and missed "Candy" when the story ended, since I had lived with her for a couple of days....

The story is interesting and very well written and should be instructive too, the way it is done - "painlessly".

My only suggestions, since it does seem to have that "instruction" angle, are in regard to terminology:

'Candy speaks of Belle as her "half-sister" when the correct term is "by the same sire". In horse language (among blood horses that is, and the Arab is certainly that) only produce from the same mare are "half-brothers" or "half-sisters" regardless of what it might be in human counterparts. This could make a good discourse in itself, and one that should make a mare proud to announce, since it is done to give distinction to a dam...who can in any case have only a few foals while a stallion can sire hundreds. So instead of a good foal having hundreds of "halfbrothers" (or -sisters) it can have only an elite few. And if they are good, the mare is truly distinguished and worthy of note.

I may be out of date or something, but I have always seen "crupper" spelled that way instead of "crouper". Is this something new?

Also, since this is supposed to be educational, the word "veterinary" should be "veterinarian", because the former is an adjective (I guess) and used as "veterinary surgeon", etc. but never just "veterinary". Never correctly, that is.

Regarding dogs, Candy mentions that "litter sister" is the same as "full sister" but it is only if the pups are from the same litter. If of later (or earlier) litters, the terminoldy is the same as with horses - "full sister".

I know you are aware of this, but since it is a pet peeve of mine I will mention it - many breeds can be "police dogs", in Germany Airedales as so used, in England Labradors are police dogs, and German Shepherds, Dobermans, etc. are also used in this work. So there is no such (recognised) breed as Police Dog, and it would give the book more authenticity if the A.K.C. name (German Shepherd) were used.

page v

2

One place did rather confuse me - in Chapter 20, page 1, Candy says her milk came in <u>four</u> streams. I have known milk to spray out in such cases, but (in mares) in only two streams - or at least a spray from both nipples. How was this "four" done?

The only other "educational" complaint I have is in regard to calling a colt a "stallion" in 2 and 3-yr classes (only I know that in some fairs and especially in the east they even call a suckling colt a "stallion" but correctly the term is "colt" until he reached four years, even if he has been used at stud. I mentioned this last because in regard to fillies, some people (when Arabian shows were started) had the archaic idea that a filly became a "mare" as soon as she had been bred. Considering some can (a be bred as yearlings, that's being a bit goofy, to make such an unreliable distinction. And how would a judge know, or what would you call a ten-year-old that had never been bred? <u>She</u> is a filly, yet? So you see why the age system is used.

These are all more or less pedantic comments to which you need not pay any attention, unless of course you want to keep up the education concept, along the line of the charts, etc.

The drawing of the "wild-haired" colt (stallion?) is intriguing too, and pictures him exactly.

Good luck with the book, and thanks again for allowing me to see it in this "preview"

Sincerely,

Gladys Edwards

List Of Pictures

Chapter 1

Oh! Mommie, Mommie, Mommie!

Now I know why the tears came to Helen's eyes when she told that Man and Lady and their daughter she would "sell" me to them. They came so often...I just thought it was lots of fun practicing my walk and trot for them. I can remember being actually glad when their daughter would go skipping past all the other stalls and stop in front of mine. She'd say, "Helen, would you take Stick O Candy out and have her practice a little bit?" Helen would smile, and say "You like my Sticky-girl?" Then she'd hug me...you know the way she does. Helen loved me so much. She loves you too, Mommie. Is your real name "Sweetie Pie"? Or is that just Helen's pet name for you.

Stick O'Candy at six months old with Helen.

She'll never sell you, Mommie...or Aunt Sugar...or Daddy-Gabbar! Gabbar's my daddy (sire) and Sweetie Pie's my mommie (dam)...how come he had more children (foals) than you do, Mommie? How come he's my Daddy and Puddin's Daddy, too! Did he marry Aunt Sugar at the same time he married you? Is Daddy a stallion? Is it a purebred Arabian stallion when you have to stay in a big box stall most of the time? And when you go outdoors you have to be all alone in a big paddock? Boy-oh-boy that Man and Lady and their Daughter sure thought Daddy-Gabbar was beautiful...and I do, too.

Will I ever see Daddy again? Will I ever see you? Or Helen? Will I ever see anyone from home again? Now that I know what "sell" means...I wish I hadn't been such a show-off. When Helen said, "Trot!" I should have planted all four feet on the ground and refused to budge. I should have laid back my ears, switched my tail around like mad. I should have switched my tail around and then glued it down to my fanny. Not me, though! I had to go and be a smart show-off. "Sell" means people fall in love with you...they fall in love with you and before you can say Jack Robinson they have you stuffed into a box on wheels and you've lost your happy home! Warn Puddin, Mommie! And warn Buggy! Tell them to act mean when strange people come to look at them. Tell them to make sure no strangers are watching them when they arch their tails and do the Arabian float. Too risky! People might fall in love with them like they did with me...and you know what that means...sell.

It wasn't easy for them, though...stuffing me into that box on wheels. It took Helen to make me get in...and that was the first time in my life that I tried to disobey my dear, darling Helen. I tried very hard to disobey...and when she

Gabbar and Helen's granddaughter, Suzette.

finally got me into the box, she hugged me and hugged me...with tears rolling down her face. Remember the time Jezebel's little foal got hurt and died? Everyone cried then, too.

I had a hard time keeping my balance when the box on wheels began to move. It jiggled under my feet. I heard that Man and Lady and their Daughter calling to Helen..."Don't worry...we'll take good care of her...we'll take wonderful care of your Stick O Candy." Every once in awhile the box would stop and the three of them would come and talk with me. Their Daughter would climb in and hug me...almost like Helen. Their Daughter sorta croons, Mommie. All three of them do. They don't seem like bad people...but why did they have to take me away from home? I used to like them when they came to watch me practice my lessons...I even liked having their Daughter lead me around. She always got such a kick out of the way I would walk when she said "Walk!" and the way I'd trot when she said "Trot!" She's thirteen years old...did you know that, Mommie?

Well anyway...when that big box finally stopped and stayed stopped...I was heavens knows how far from home. Have you ever been jiggled in a box on wheels, Mommie? Not too bad when you get used to it...but I was glad to get my feet on the ground again. That Man said, "Run to the barn, Honey! Turn on the lights for this little Candy-baby." I guess their Daughter's name is "Honey". Do you like that for a name? She dashed on ahead of us and that Man said, "This is your new home, Candy-girl. A nice, cheery barn...with a cozy box stall...and see the pretty wooden fence around your barn? You'll be just like your Daddy, with a paddock of your very own.

That Man did every thing he could to make me like the place. He sweet-talked me all the way up the driveway, all the way around the house, and through the gate in the white board fence. It was pitch dark when we got here...wherever "here" is. I could see Honey standing in a pool of light at the door of the barn. I want-ed to reach down and nibble a little bit of the soft, dewy grass...but I was curi-ous about the "cozy box stall."

Sally Dog and relatives.

There's even a radio in this barn, Mommie. And I guess they leave it turned on all the time. It is a cheery place to be...and that Man and Lady and Honey do a lot of talking. Honey rattles along a mile a minute...and that Man seems to smile most of the time. He smiles and says, "You're going to be all right,Candy-girl. We've wanted a little dolly like you for a long, long time." It does help quite a bit...having them talk to me all the time like they do. Every two minutes, Honey would say, "Do you think Stick O'Candy will like it here?"

Maybe I will like it, and maybe I won't! Right this minute all I can think of is how terribly lonely I am. It's morning now...I can look out the window and see the sun coming up and shining on things I've never seen before. I don't even want to look. I want to shut my eyes tight and see my own world come true again. I can do it, too! I can shut my eyes and see all of us there at home in the morning at this time...waiting for Helen to come. Or maybe she's already there. Are you already eating your breakfast? Are there tears running down Helen's face? Does everybody miss me? Do you think

Puddin and Buggy will be able to have fun without me? Probably not...probably they won't even feel like playing at all...huh? You and Aunt Sugar won't either...will you? And I know Daddy-Gabbar won't. When Helen puts him out in his paddock to play, he'll just stand around as quiet as a mouse. He won't even run up and down the hills with his neck arched and his mane and tail flying in the wind. Will he Mommie? Will he?

I don't even have any breakfast. And if anybody brings me any breakfast I won't even eat it! This is a darn ole' barn. This is a darn ole' barn with a darn ole' box stall...and a darn ole' radio with a darn ole' man saying, "It's a beautiful sunshiny morning." Beautiful! Phooie! The darn ole' birds are singing their dumb heads off...a rooster is crowing at the top of his lungs...and there's a darn ole' cow mooing. Darn ole' cow! She's hungry...that's what. Nobody feeds anybody around this darn ole' place. I'll probably starve before they even remember I'm in this barn. They won't remember me for twenty-one weeks, and I'll be skinny-as-a-rail-dead. That's what I'll be...skinny as a rail and starved to death!

Now there's a dog barking it's head off. Go on, dog...bark your head off! They won't feed you either. Poor hungry dog. Poor, poor hungry dog...poor, poor, hungry, hungry dog...dog. Poor Stick O'Candy's what I should be saying. If I cried, would tears run down my face like people? Tears are made out of water.

Mommie the water here is delicious. There's a great big bucket of it here in my box stall...and whenever I get thirsty I just walk right over and take a nice, big drink! What's really fun is to walk right over and get a big mouthful and let it dribble down your chin...or walk right over and stick your face in it and splash. Boy-oh-boy, my bucket is almost empty it's so much fun.

This ole' mental telepathy game you taught me is fun, too. Now that I'm so far away, you'll probably hear from me often. I have to stop now, though...I can hear Honey calling that dog. She's bringing that barking dog to the barn!

Chapter 2

Hey Mommie! I jumped three fences yesterday!

Three high fences. Right after breakfast, that Man and Lady wanted to clean my stall...so Honey took me out in my paddock. Sally (the dog) had to sit and watch, while I walked and trotted on the lead rope. I get a kick out of Honey...she always calls me "Candy"...in fact none of them seem to remember that my pet-name has always been "Sticky."

That Man and Lady had a wheel barrel parked by my barn door...and when Honey turned me loose, I went over to see if they were doing a good job on my box stall. There was piece of board propping the door open, and it got caught in my tail when I laid down to roll. The board was hanging on my tail when I stood up, and it scared me to death! I began to run...and the board banged my legs...I was terrified! The faster I ran, the harder it banged. I jumped out of my paddock...turned around and jumped back in...ran all the way across and jumped out the other side. When I dodged between some trees, the board got pulled off...and when it stopped banging my legs, I stopped running. Stood still as a mouse until Honey and that Man found me...and I've never been so glad to see anyone in my whole life. They almost carried me back to my cozy box stall.

I had been so frightened I was almost black with sweat. The veterinarian came and gave me a shot, to keep infection away. I didn't have any scratches from the fences, because I'm such a good jumper...just scratches where the board banged me. This veterinarian had a neat way of giving shots. You think he's just giving you some quick pats on the fanny...you don't even feel it when the needle goes in. After the needle is in, he screws the medicine tube onto it...and the shot is over and done with before you have time to fuss.

He liked me. He said, "This little filly has plenty of good old horse sense. Notice how she responds to the tone of your voice? She's still quivering...but she knows she's safe now." And I did feel safe. I'm glad I'm a little filly with plenty of good old horse sense...was I born with it? He said most horses are born with horse sense, but some don't learn to use it. Then he gave me a pat, and said, "You don't have to worry about this young lady...beautiful outside, horse sense inside...a perfect combination." Would I sound more grown up if I called you "mother" instead of "Mommie?"

Maybe I use my horse sense because you set such a good example, Mother. Remember the time when I was being weaned? Remember the "temporary partition" Helen put between us? Bob-oh-boy that thing was really temporary. It came loose the very first night! You had to prop it up from your side, and I had to prop it up from ny side. Helen practically laughed her head off when she found us "holding up the wall" the next morning. She used to tell everyone about it and say how smart we were...she said lots of horses would have gone stark-raving-mad if the walls caved in on them. My new family knows about that temporary wall, and they told the veterinarian.

Honey was thrilled with Stick O'Candy.

He said, "That figures. When a mare has reasoning-power, she usually passes it on to her offspring...a foal can pick up a lot of things from it's dam during those months of nursing." He stayed here quite awhile...said he likes to have his "patients" feel like he's a friend.

My big bucket of water looks mighty inviting right now but I want to finish telling you this stuff before breakfast. I still miss you like sixty, but there's never a dull moment around this place. I got better acquainted with my family yesterday because at least one of them was with me all day long. That Man's name is "Mister" and the Lady's name is "Missus" I think they have another name on the end, but I can't remember what that is. There's Mister, Missus, Honey, Sally-dog, and a cat named "Tatty-Put."

Lots of people came to look at me yesterday afternoon. Did you know I'm three-fourths Arabian and one-fourth American Saddlebred...and I'm a yearling? They're going to take me to a Horse Show sometime, because I'm a "terrific specimen." They won't leave me at the Horse Show, though...they'll bring me right back home after a "judge" looks at me. I'd rather have the "judge" come here to look at me. I'll get stuffed into the box-on-wheels again...but I guess they don't call it a box...they call it a "horse trailer." A "horse trailer" is for "travelling."

One man who came visiting said, "You won't be wanting this crazy little character. She jumps all the fences...she splashes water all over...I'll do you a big favor, and take her off your hands." Mister laughed, and said, "You old horse-trader...there isn't enough money in the world to buy this little gal...you're wasting your time, boy." Honey said, "We won't ever sell the Candy horse...she wouldn't be happy with anyone else!" The Missus said, "Hear that, you fellows? Candy's already a member of the family!" It went on like that all afternoon...just like Sundays when all the people would come to see Daddy, at Helen's place.

In the evening we had a terrible rain storm full of thunder and lightening. Mister said, "Lordy! Poor little Candy is getting a fancy introduction to her new home. She must think her world has turned upside down...with that board banging her all over the lot this morning, and now the heavens letting loose with a cloudburst!" Storms haven't bothered me much, though...not even the bad ones like last night.

Missus brought "TV dinners" out to my barn and we all ate at the same time. My box stall takes up one-third of the barn...then there's a "tack room" with a table and some chairs...and next comes the room where they keep the hay and straw. I feel like I'm right with them in the "tack room", the dividing wall, just comes up to my "withers." In case you don't know where your withers are, Mother...just turn your head around and see where the hair of your mane comes to an end on your back, and that's the place to find them. Your withers should be prominent. Your withers should be just as high as your fanny...only your fanny isn't your fanny... it's your "croup." Whew! I'm learning a lot of new words. Your croup should be quite level...with your tail attached nice and high.

They had a book about Arabian horses out here last night, and Missus kept pointing at different parts of me that I've never ever heard of before. One thing it says in that book is that many people can't look at a whole horse all at once. Doesn't that strike your funny bone? It says some people can't see anything but the head...some can't see anything but the neck...some can't see anything but the withers, or the croup, or the legs...or a million other separate pieces. The book says people should learn all the separate pieces, but what really counts is all of them put together. Naturally!

I can see right now that there's a lot about horses even I don't know...and I am a horse. How about you, Mother? Do you think your front leg is just your front leg? Ha! Your front leg has all these things in it.

Chapter 3

Say, Mother...before I forget...

Tell Puddin and Buggy I take it all back about how horrible it is to be sold. In my case anyway, it's turning out to be a heck of a lot of fun. I can honestly say that I love my new home. I love Mister and Missus and Honey and Sally, and even little Tatty-Put I love. He's a sweet cat...with long fluffy hair. He likes to have Missus drape him around her shoulders like a fur-piece...comical to watch. He wears a red collar, and walks around like a little puppy-dog.

We just have a half-acre here...and the family worries a lot about all the traffic going to and from the Country Club, which is right next door. The golf course is near my paddock...and Honey's Grandfather positively dotes on that game. He plays every day, and once in awhile he comes over to visit with me. He teases Honey...says, "That great big wild horse of yours bit me the other day." Or, "Candy must be going into the Sport Shop business. The fellows at the Club tell me she keeps jumping fences and grabbing their golf balls." Honey "bites" on his little jokes. She says, "Dinpop! Candy loves fresh meat...you shouldn't begrudge her a little bite now and then." Or, "tell those fellows at the Club it's "finders-keepers" with their old golf balls...Candy grabs them for me to play jacks with.

Her "Dinpop" is quite a man. He used to live on a farm with a horse and buggy. He'd taken a girl to a dance, and tied his horse to a tree...when the dance was over he discovered his horse had untied the knot and gone home. Sounds a wee bit far-fetched, but he swears up and down that his horse could untie any knot he invented. Honey loves to hear him tell about old times...and how smart that horse was.

It was Dinpop who got Honey up on a real-life horse for the first time...back during World War II, when Mister was in the Navy. She was just a little tyke then...Dinpop came over to play with her whenever he had time. They lived in town then...and she used to listen to Roy Rogers all the time. Roy and a horse named "Trigger" made all the kids "cowboy conscious."

Our house, (I mean their house, because that was long before they had me) had a big old-fashioned porch with a railing...just right to "ride" on. If it was nice outdoors, Honey and a little girl friend would ride on the railing...and when it was raining, the kitchen chairs went galloping through the house. Missus says she could expect anything in those days...from "Indian ambushes" to "wild horse round-ups." Then one fine day, the completely unexpected arrived! Dinpop in the front yard on a real, live horse! He took Honey for a "tandem pair" ride on the rented horse...and from then on, it was, "When can we get a horse, when can we get a horse, when can we get a horse!" From morning 'til night.

When Mister came home from the Navy, they got Sally-dog...but she didn't cure the horse-fever. They got Tatty-Put, and he didn't cure it either. An honest-to-goodness saddle became a permanent fixture on the banister in the living room...Dinpop brought the rented horse around occasionally...Honey and her girl friend took turns "driving" each other to school...and with all that "exposure"...they finally bought a horse.

Sally-dog.

Mister and Missus say the world is full of horses "any kid could ride." They say the horse-traders that palm them off on unsuspecting parents should be tarred and feathered. All in all, they bought and sold four horses "any kid could ride" before they got wise. After they stocked some good feed into those "starved rodeo stock" they were brought back to "bucking-good-condition." Mister says, "There's nothing like good nourishment for bringing out the worst in a horse." They laugh about it now...but they were plenty sad about it then.

They had even moved to this half-acre so it would be possible to keep a horse, and they were terribly disappointed when each one turned out to be dangerous after it plumped up a bit. One man even concealed the fact that the horse he was selling them was a confirmed "run-away." It was a beautiful American Saddlebred...and was just fine for a few days. Out of a clear blue sky, it ran away with Honey...and heaven knows how she was able to stop it. When they telephoned the former owner, he told them to contact the man who had trained it. When they telephoned the trainer, he was flabbergasted. He said, "Do you mean to tell me that horse was sold for a child to ride?" He told them he had shown the horse for the owner for three years...and he never knew when the horse would run away with one of his professional riders! Sometimes it performed beautifully...and other times, that run-away quirk would come out. Isn't that awful? Tar and feathers would be too good for a man who would sell that kind of horse to a child.

So the first time they came to Helen's place, they were shopping for dependable, "well-fed" riding horse. Helen didn't have any riding horses for sale, but she showed them all her Arabians anyway. The second time they came, it was for second look at Puddin, Buggy and yours truly. Even though

Honey beaming on an "out-law" on good feed.

we were too young to be trained for riding, they couldn't resist temptation...and you know the story from then on.

Don't let on to Puddin and Buggy, but I think I was Helen's special pet. She really wanted to keep me, and sell one of them...didn't she Mommie. I mean Mother. Didn't she? But Mister and Missus and Honey fell in love with me, me, me. Wasn't it cute the way Honey would go skipping past all the other stalls, and stop in front of mine? She'd say, "Helen, would you take Stick O'Candy out and have her practice a little bit?" I could just kiss Helen for hugging me and saying, "You like my little Sticky-girl?" I was really her pet. I'm sure of it.

Gee whizz, the time goes fast. School is open now, so Missus and I are at home alone during most of the say. We have a little game we play together...at least Missus calls it a game. When you're the only horse in the family, you really like to have the people talk to you...and you get in the habit of answering them. I'm outdoors often, and usually keep one eye on the house...which is about a hundred feet from my fence. Missus comes to the window and calls, "Candy! Say a little word." I whinny...and she says, "That's a good little Candy-girl." Sometimes when they have company, we do it to "show how smart Candy is."

I've learned more out of that Arabian book, Mother. Remember the name of all the things in your front legs? Well, the other night I learned that we Arabian horses don't arch our tails high just for fun...we're supposed to do it. Our croups are supposed to have a natural arch. The book says it happens many times that "crossbreds" have unusually pronounced Arabian characteristics. I do...and I'm a crossbred...because part of me is pure Arabian, and the rest of me is pure American Saddlebred. It's a very interesting book....and if you were amazed at how many pieces are in your front legs, you'll think your back one has a hundred-million for sure.

Chapter 4

There's a new "boarder" in my barn, Mother!

It's a big, strange tom cat with bushy gray fur. He comes right into my stall and snuggles down in the straw to sleep. I kind'a like to have him here, but Missus says, "No more cats!" He doesn't pay one speck of attention to that kind of talk, though...and Missus figures as long as he hangs around our place, he might as well have a little food. He goes up to the house every evening for a "hand-out"...and the rest of the time he stays near me. You ought to see the way he pounces on a mouse! Whammo!

He's a regular tag-along. When Honey has me practice walking and trotting, she has to keep telling him to stay out from under my feet. When Missus is at the clothesline hanging up sheets and stuff...she has to stumble all over him while he rubs around her ankles. He purrs so loud I bet they can hear him way over at the Country Club. Mister comes out and says, "Is this a new pal, Candy-girl?" He picks him up and cuddles him...and once I heard him say, "You old pile of gray stuff! The lady of this ranch says we can't have any more cats...where did you come from, anyway?"

Just between you and me and the gate-post, that little furry beasty is here to stay...no matter what Missus might say. I think she's afraid he'll hurt Tatty-put, but he wouldn't hurt a flea...Gray Stuffy likes us...he wants to be part of our family. Honey and Sally-dog want him to stay...Mister wants him to stay...I want him to stay...and even if Missus says she wants him to go away, I notice he has a dish of milk whenever he looks hungry. Women are funny, aren't they.

Mister says he's outnumbered by females around here...and another tomcat would help even things up. Mister's favorite expression is "Women!" To hear him say it, you'd think he couldn't stand women...but I know better. He hardly lets Missus out of his sight when he's at home...calls her his girl bride. He always does nice things for Honey...thinks Sally is the best dog in the whole wide world....and he calls me his new little girl. He may say "Women!" all the time but he wouldn't trade his women for all the tea in China...I'd bet my bottom dollar on it.

Golly, there's a lot of snow this winter. Do you have big drifts of it there, too? We have to buy all the hay and straw we use, and we don't have a place to store a whole winter's supply...so we have the farmer bring it when we run out. The farmer was suppose to bring hay the day before Thanksgiving, but we had such a blizzard he couldn't even get the wagon out of his barn. Mister and Missus and Honey got all bundled up and took Honey's sled to the farm for a few bales to tide us over. They took Sally

Helen Sinclair and Gabbar at Sinclair Arabians in Hayward, Minnesota

along, but Mister has to end up carrying her because the snow was so deep...and they looked like a bunch of snowmen when they got back. Missus and Honey said they were the ones with the hard job...pulling the sled full of hay!

I'm not trained for it yet, but we have a little old-fashioned sleigh, Mother. A real one...with red plush seats, and little doors on each side that open and shut. They brought it from a man who had it safely stored in a barn for almost sixty years. We're just sick about the way it's getting ruined by the weather, through. My barn isn't big enough to store it in...and the garage is full of automobiles. Honey says she wishes we could have it like it was in those days Dinpop tells about...when the people rode around in buggies and sleighs. He gave her the jinglebells he used to use, and at Christmas time they were hanging on my barn door. When the wind blew, they jingled and jingled.

I'm "officially" two years old, now...but I won't really be two until the twelfth of June. My "official" birthday was last week...on the first day of January. Isn't it funny to have two birthdays every year? The "official" one and the really-honest-to-goodness one? Mister says it has something to do with race-horses at race-tracks. A silly business, to my way of thinking...but then I'm not a race-horse. Mister says nobody-but-nobody will ever be allowed to race me. He says racing ruins a lot of horses...because once a horse gets a taste of racing, it wants to race all the time...and that does it.

I don't see how any horse can race in all this snow...it's all I can do to just walk in it. I'm anxious for spring to come, but it was nice having snow for Christmas. So sparkling and clean...the radio playing Christmas songs all the time...and me, cozy and warm with bright dry straw way up to my knees. Isn't clean straw in a box stall beautiful at night when all the lights are turned on? It says in the book that it doesn't matter how cold the weather is, a horse can stay healthy if it can stay dry. You need dry bedding...and you shouldn't be in a draft...but your barn should have good ventilation so the steam from your breath and your body can get out. If your steam can't get out, the barn will get "clammy"...and clammy can even make you get pneumonia...pretty bad stuff, that clammy and pneumonia.

I'm glad I have clean, dry straw...and I'm glad my barn has good ventilation! I stay inside during cold, blizzardy weather...on sunshiny days I can go out as much as I please. When it's sleeting or blizzarding, they shut my door...my family isn't spoiling me, Mother...it just sounds like they are. Ha!

Pity the poor horses who don't have anyone to take care of them...the poor ones that have to stand outside in all kinds of weather. Cold, rain, sleet, blizzards...with not even a roof to huddle under. The tears came to Honey's eyes the other night when they were talking about it. She loves all animals, Mother. From stray little gray tomcats to any animal you could mention in the whole world. Missus says Honey has compassion for all God's creatures, and she wouldn't want her to be any other way. Is compassion like love? I think it is. Honey wants all the people and all the animals to be safe...even if they're not very nice. Do you know what "The Ten Commandments" are, Mother? They're in a book, a book named "The Bible."

And speaking of books...our book about Arabian horses is plumb full of important information. There's the clammy that I just told you about...the names off all those pieces of your front and back legs...and just in case you're wondering, dear Mother...you have a list of things in your head about ten miles long.

Chapter 5

hee! We're getting another horse...and we're moving!

How's that for news in a nutshell? I can hardly wait for it all to happen...and the way it sounds, I won't have to wait long.

How it started, was a good friend of the family came to visit, and said, "What's your Honey going to do for a riding horse while Candy's growing up? I have just the horse you need...and she's for sale. Shall I bring her out?" He has two he'd like to bring out, but only one of them is trained for riding. They're Appaloosa mares...full sisters...and "gentle as lambs." He knows about the family's tough luck with those old broncos...and says Honey will be able to ride "Sherezade" any day of the year, without us having to worry one speck. She's been a broodmare-riding-horse for him, and he wants her to go to a good home. Sherezade is a pretty name...don't you think so, Mother? It's too bad to have to separate the sisters, but like I said...Sherezade is the only one trained for riding.

She had a foal this spring, so she won't be able to leave until along in the fall when it's weaned...and by that time we'll have ten whole acres to run around in. Honey calls her "Sherry"...and goes over to ride her several times a week. She says the little foal is cute as a button...white, with black spots all over. When Honey rides Sherry, the baby goes romping along right beside them...can't understand why it's mother "wears" a human being on her back...tee hee. It gets the toes of Honey's boots wet with it's little mouth...and one time the little dickens used its teeth on the skirt of her saddle.

Appaloosa horses were famous "war horses" for the Nez Perce Indians. They were fast runners, and when the United States soldiers were fighting the Indians, the Nez Perce tribe was able to hold out for a long time on account of their nimble horses. The Nez Perce tribe used "very intelligent breeding principles." If stallions weren't just about perfect, they were gelded...and the inferior specimens were traded off to other tribes. History has it that Appaloosa horses "were imported to Mexico in about sixteen-hundred...with shipments of goods from the Near East or Spain." I guess Appaloosas have some Arabian blood in them, and when the Nez Perce got their hands on them, they fell in love with them, lock, stock and barrel. With their superior breeding know-how, they "bred them into a distinct type, during the hundred years between seventeen-thirty and eighteen-thirty." We have a little book about Appaloosas, and that's what it says.

The Appaloosa book says the Nez Perce loved to race their horses, and maybe all that practice was what helped them get away from the soldiers in the fights. They used the Appaloosas for war, racing, and "buffalo hunting." I'd like to see a buffalo sometime...Honey says she hasn't seen any face-to-face, but in pictures they have withers that are higher than their heads. She giggled, but I think it sounds awful...withers higher than your head...icky icky icky! Wonder how high their croups are!

Honey and Sherry going "western".

Sherry will be for "Western" riding...and when I grow up I'm going to be for both "Western" and "English." I can't figure it out. They say when you're for English, everything has to be very proper...and the riders wear flat-heeled, round-toed boots. For Western, they wear high-heeled, pointed boots...so I s'pose they're improper. I'm sure anxious to get a look at Sherry.

At our new place we're going to have a bigger barn and a huge pasture. Out in the pasture we'll have a three-sided shelter house to get into and out of whenever we please. It'll have a roof...and whenever it rains or anything we can just pop right in there and be snug as bugs in a rug. The barn will have a hayloft upstairs and three big box stalls downstairs, even though we just need two. It'll be like a house with a spare bedroom. We're going to have a lot of cleaning up to do...even some old ramshackly buildings to tear down. We'll probably have to hire some help if we're going to have things ship-shape by the time Sherry comes to live with us.

Page 16

I'll kinda miss this little barn and paddock...but I don't have to miss Gray Stuffy...she's going right along with us. Did you notice I said she instead of he? We found that out when she had a litter of kittens in my box

Honey with two of Grey Stuffy's kittens.

stall. Right in my stall, mind you! Mister howled, "Gray Stuff! You sold me out! Now the boys on this ranch are really out-numbered!" Mother I hate to tell you this, but a short time after that, little Tatty-put died...and now Mister is the only boy. Tatty-put was very, very dear...and I guess I won't talk about how much we miss that little cat.

Missus will be glad to leave this half-acre. She hasn't liked it since she found out how crammed a certain ranch-style house could be...about ten minutes after the last load of furniture was transported from the house in town. That house (in town) had a full basement, two full stories, plus a big attic with a real stairway up to it. This house has one floor, period. No basement...and it might as well not have an attic, because they have to crawl up through a hole in the ceiling to get there. There's not much space outdoors, either. Half an acre is pretty teeny when you get out in the coun-try. Live and learn, they say...but with ten acres we'll have oceans of room to run around in.

I don't know very much about the new house. I think it's big enough, but the problem seems to be how to make it decent enough to live in...can it possibly be that bad? Missus says she can fix it up...and "Anything will be better than this crackerbox." Have you ever heard of "claustrophobia," Mother? It sounds as bad as clammy, and I don't blame her for wanting to move. She says the walls are too close together...and they have to go outside to turn around. I can turn around in my box stall as easy as pie, so I'm better off than the family. Sometimes I turn around three or four times before I lie down to rest...like Sally does.

Oh...about Gray Stuff's kittens. We gave them all away...to one of the ladies who works at the office with Mister. We waited until they were weaned, and their names were Poke-bonnet...Calico-bunny...Midnight...and Stinky. Stuffy is definitely our cat now, and everyone just loves her to pieces. The tips of her ears are round instead of pointed...we think they must have frozen and crumbled off a long time ago. She looks cute with her little round ears, and now we think cats with pointed ears look strange. She's round all over...and such bushy, bushy fur!

One thing I hope...I hope the family come out to the new barn just as often as they come out to this one. I love to be brushed and fussed over. I'm anxious to get moved and have Sherry here for company, too. Know how old she is? She's nine and her sister, Manitoba, is four. Wish we could get Manitoba...then I'd have someone to chum with when Honey's riding Western.

Sherezade, Jezebel and Ibn Gabbar in the pasture.

Mister says it takes more "elbow grease" to keep a white horse clean...harder to make 'em shine, too. I'm a chestnut, and I'm clean and shiny all the time. Mother, have you studied your lessons like a good girl? There are a few pieces of horse that I haven't mentioned before.

Chapter 6

The time has just skittered along, Mother Mia.

Mia" is "mine...in Spanish. Honey calls Missus that once in awhile, and I kind'a like the sound of it. Some of Sherry's ancestors came from Spain so she'll be speaking Spanish quite often...wouldn't you think? Does daddy speak Arabian much? How come I don't know how? I can speak American for my one-fourth American Saddlebred, but I don't know anything about horses' names for my three-fourths Arabian. What will Sherry think of that!

I said the time skittered...and really mean it. We're moved to our new ten-acre place and Sherry will come next Tuesday. The barn is all finished and the big pasture is delicious...I go out there for snacks everyday. That three-sided shelter barn is quite a deal. I've already used it three times when it rained. Stood in there big as you please, and not one rain-drop touched me. I've even used it several times when the sun was too hot. This may sound strange, but we're going to let the manure build up on the floor of the pasture barn...for warmth for our "tootsies" this winter. I'm anxious for Sherry to come and help me "lay the carpet," but Mister says we can't start the carpet until after we're both wormed.

My poor family! They have everything fixed up fine for the live-stock...and now they're trying to get the home finished. Mister took a good look and said, "Ye Gods! It's a hopeless proposition!" At least it had a bathroom by the time they moved in, and Missus had the kitchen painted. Except for the plumbing and heating and some carpenter work, it will be a do-it-yourself modeling job. Missus has all kinds of "plans"...and Mister says that's what scares him. When he said, "Don't you worry your head, I can do it all by myself!"...he said, "Yup. Like the time you were going to refinish that house-full of woodwork all by yourself! Women!"

That was before they had me, but he reminds her of it so often I know the whole story. They bought a house that needed some remodeling, as usual, and while the carpenters were busy moving walls around, Missus decided to wash all the woodwork

Now that I'm getting older, I'm finding more things that I enjoy doing. With summer vacation over and Honey back in school, I'm alone more in the day time. Missus is busy in the house...refinishing the woodwork...and I've learned how to be a do-it-yourselfer, too. Began thinking about all the things that Dinpop's horse did, and discovered I'm not so dumb either.

The other day, it was exciting. Our lay-out at this place has the barn about one hundred feet from the house, a wood-rail paddock beside the barn, and the big pasture is behind both the barn and the paddock. I'm very seldom in the house yard (when I'm there, it's always on a lead rope) and the grass there has a greener flavor. The other day I was in the paddock looking over the fence at that grass...wishing I could have a few nibbles...when I thought of trying my hand at opening the gate.

Easy as pie! All you have to do is slide a two-by-four back out of a slot...and the gate swings open right now. Had it figured out in no time, and when Mister came home for lunch he was amazed to find me loose in the yard. I wasn't ready to be caught yet, so when he came to get me I kept edging away. Soon I was in the driveway...out the drive and onto the road...a car whizzed past me, and I began to run. Hadn't ever been out on the road before, and I was halfway scared. I must have been a quarter of a mile from home, when I saw a car coming toward me...and then I was really afraid. I whirled around to run away from it, and golly knows how far I would have gone...but I noticed Mister waving his arms and calling my name. I was glad enough to skid at right-angles and gallop back to home base...right back through the gate I had opened.

The next day when I worked on that gate, there was a rope tying it shut. I managed to make sort of a fringe out of the rope...but couldn't untie the knot. I examine the gate every day now to see if they've forgotten to put the rope there...all I want is to be able to go out exploring when the mood strikes me. I really don't want to go out on that road again...unless I'm in a trailer going to a Horse Show or something. It will be better when Sherry comes...we can play together...and she's so much older than I am, maybe she knows how to untie knots.

Chapter 7

Sherry's just like you, Mother.

But gee I felt sorry for her when she first came. Had to leave her little baby at home, you know...she really worried about it. A nursing foal beside her one day, then boomo...into the trailer and off to a new home without an I, yes, or no. The baby was five months old...big and healthy...but she missed it so much. How would you feel if your baby followed every step that you took for five months and then all of a sudden you couldn't find it anymore! I'm glad I was weaned with that temporary wall between you and me. Heck, I was six months old and didn't need the milk anymore...it was you I needed. Missus said when I grow up and have a baby they'll let us be close enough to smell each other and talk to each other when it's time for weaning. Poor Sherry was practically beside herself for two or three days.

When she began to take an interest in things here...that's when the fun began. The human beings in the family weren't brand new to her like Sally and Stuffy and I were. She liked Sally right off the bat...but Gray Stuff! She's such a bushy little gadget...and probably Sherry hadn't ever seen a round-eared cat before. The first time Stuffy hopped up to the feed opening of Sherry's stall I thought the old gal was going to jump out of her boots. She opened her eyes a mile wide and stared at the cat in disbelief!

Her feet were rooted to the floor...and she showed her early Arabian blood by flattening her croup and arching her tail. Just as unconcerned as ever, Stuffy jumped down and purred like a motor boat while she rubbed around on Sherry's legs. I didn't say a word...just kept peeking between the boards of the wall. Whenever the cat rubbed, Sherry's eyes followed...then after a few minutes it was just as if she thought, "Oh well, whatever it is, it's harmless." She'd even reach down and nudge Stuffy with her nose after that.

Nothing seems to bother her very much. That friend of the family really meant it when he said Sherry was gentle as a lamb...it was really a good deed when he sold her to us. Mister and Missus say, "Why, oh why couldn't someone have sold us a horse like Sherry in the beginning." They wonder if many other people have to learn about horses and "horse-traders" the hard way. We're glad she's pretty to look at...but even ugly as mud, her wonderful disposition would make her worth a fortune to parents wanting a really dependable horse for a child. We'll always have a soft spot in our hearts for that fine, fine gentleman who wanted Honey to have a riding horse she would always enjoy.

Remember when I thought Western riding would be improper because English was supposed to be proper? Well it just goes to show how easy it is to make boo-boos when you really don't know what you're talking about. English and Western are both proper...both very exact...and it's good for a horse to be trained both ways, like I'm going to be.

Honey and Sherry in a costume class line up.

They say when a person is riding English, both hands are busy with the reins...but in Western, one hand holds the reins and the other is free. Most people hold Western reins in their left hand...but there's no hard and fast rule about it. Honey is very right-handed, and says she feels "out of gear" trying to hold the Western reins in her left hand. Anyway...when she rides Sherry, there's always one hand free to "rope a steer"...ha! That'll be the day! Honey roping a steer, for heaven's sake.

Tell that to Puddin and Buggy, Mother. Tell them Western has one hand free to rope a steer...and English has both hands busy steering the horse. Except (and this'll throw'em) when it's cross country English, "in which case the rider holds four reins in one hand." Whew! Four reins in one hand! I think that's just for when Gulliver travels cross country. Sure like to see that Gulliver. They say he's so big he can step right over a barn...and what I'd like to know is why the heck he goes around riding cross country on horses that are smaller than the barn! The big bully!

Ha! Honey should have long legs like Gulliver. The she could stand up and walk when Sherry trots. She says her rear end "takes a real beating," and no matter how hard she tries to stick in the saddle...she usually has to give up and start "posting." What "posting" is, is beyond me! We have a lot of posts holding up the fences but I can't see what they have to do with riding a horse. All I know is, posting doesn't beat her rear end...and not posting does.

Since Sherry came, I've had a "problem." I have it when Honey leaves me in the barn alone when she takes Sherry out for a ride. It makes me yell my head off, paw the floor, kick the sides of my stall, and it made me put my front feet in the manger...until Mister took it out. He says I'm trying to tear the barn down. But they don't understand. They don't understand that my problem is all their fault. I have to make all the commotion because I don't want to stay in the barn while those two are out having fun, and if they'd take me along...my problem would go away.

I remember Honey telling about Sherry's baby going along when she rode Western...and she thought it was "just precious." Heck...she hardly knew that baby. It wasn't a member of the family, and I am. I'd just walk along like a perfect lady...I wouldn't go biting at her toes like that darn ole' baby did. I'm not trying to tear the barn down on purpose...and if they'd just see this "problem" from my point of view, everything would be hunky-dory. No fuss...no muss.

Mother do you realize Christmas is just ten days away? And do you realize I'll be three years old on the first of January? Officially? The days are so short now...dark at breakfast, light for lunch, and pitch dark again for our evening meal. Where does the sun go all the time!

We don't have very much snow...and Honey says we need big piles of it for Santa Claus and his sleigh. He uses reindeer instead of horses to pull it...eight of them. He has a huge sleigh. Mister has a lovely poem about Christmas...about mice being very quiet between downstairs ceiling and the upstairs floor...about Honey hanging her stockings up by the chimney to dry...about a bunch of children with sugar-plums for heads...about Missus running around in a nightshirt, and Mister putting his brains in a cap...and he hears a big noise outside and he runs to the window and throws up his hash. Honey always chases him out of the barn before he finishes his poem, so I never get to hear it all at the same time.

Once he got back in the barn and shouted about reindeer pawing holes in the roof and a peddler falling through with a jelly belly and a sooty fur coat on. He said the peddler wouldn't even speak to anybody. Just opened a big sack and threw junk all over...then stuck his finger in his nose and went up the chimney in smoke...whistling. That was just more of his poem...that's why he didn't call the police.

Chapter 8

The "groundhog" saw his shadow today, Mother.

That means all the snow has to be gone in six weeks. Or no...it means we'll have six weeks of new snow piled on the snow we already have. Or does it mean winter will last six weeks longer than it should? Maybe I should come right out and admit I haven't the faintest idea what it means...but I did hear Mister explaining it to Honey. All kinds of stuff about six weeks, winter, old timers, tradition...and it's very important because they have headlines in the paper about it every year.

Anyway, I hope I don't have six more weeks of snow. Poor little Prinka would get lost in it. You know about Prinka? She's the new puppy we got from Santa Claus. Only four weeks old, then...and the first time I saw her she was bundled up in a doll blanket...in Honey's arms. Prinka is a purebred Scotch Collie tri-color...black, white, and tan. When she grows up she'll she'll be about twice as big as Sally-dog, because Sally is a "Border Collie."

Shall I tell you what Prinka's registered name is? Now listen carefully. Her name is Princess of Candyhorse Farm! Does that ring a bell? My family named this ten-acre place in honor of your ever loving daughter! Maybe sometime we'll put up a sign...with sticks o' candy for trimming...get it? Nobody ever calls me by my full name though...just Candy...or the Candyhorse. And I can just hear someone calling Prinka by her full name! "Here, Princess of Candyhorse Farm...Here, Princess of Candyhorse Farm!" Sally has a real whopper, too...Dilly Dally Sally...from a storybook Honey liked when she was a little girl.

Have you noticed that the days are getting nice and long? The longest day of the year is the twenty-first of June, and the shortest day is the twenty-first of December...I think. And Groundhog Day is on the one side of the middle. My personal birthday is one of the long days and my official birthday is one of the short days. In the book, it says most foals come at night...did I? Was I foaled in the moonshine or the sunshine? Mares like to have "privacy" when they foal...they like "the sheltering screen of darkness." Back when horses were wild, and didn't have any people to take care of them, the "mortality rate" was high among the babies...and mothers, too...because the herds of wild horses has to run away from so many fierce animals and things. Sometimes a mare and foal couldn't run...at least not fast enough to keep up with the herd...and fierce animals would pounce them like Gray Stuffy pounces on a mouse. Sometimes there would be a river to cross...and if it was cold weather, the little foals couldn't get dry soon enough to stay healthy. Mister says it was "survival of the fittest" in those days. Only the hardiest of the animals grew to maturity. Mother...I'm like Honey...I wish all of God's creatures could be safe and happy. Why couldn't they be, then? And why can't they be, now?

Prinka in the kitchen.

The other day Mister met a man who said, "My horses are tough. They can really take it. They're out in the corn field from picking time 'till planting." Golly, Mother...for water they have to eat snow...and for food, they have to paw down through the snow hunting for stray kernels of corn dropped by the cornpicker. The man said, "Sure...they're a little ganted-up in the spring...but mosta you guys keep your horses too fat. Turn 'em out to take care of themselves like nature intended, and they'd starve to death." Honey said, "What did you say, Daddy?" And Mister said he just asked the fellow if he'd read any good horse books lately.

We learn things from books and magazines. The fancy metal hay racks are gone from our stalls because Missus read a good article with the title, "Let Them Look Down On Their Hay." A veterinarian wrote it. I can't remember the exact, scientific reason why horses should stretch their necks down to the ground when they eat hay...but I can tell you why I like it better on the ground. You know those little green leaves in hay? Alfalfa hay? Well when my hay was in a rack, the leaves fell into my nose and eyes...never into my mouth. I didn't even know what they tasted like until they began serving my hay on the floor in a special corner of my stall. I just love the hay leaves...and Missus says they're a very important part of our nourishment. She says, "Anyone who handles good hay carelessly is throwing vitamins away." We get just a certain size wafer with each meal...and to me, brome grass is good...timothy is good...and the alfalfa part is yum, yum yummie. Between meals when I feel like a little treat, I go to my hay corner and hunt for little leaf tidbits.

It won't be long before we can stretch our necks down to the ground and eat early spring grass...what a beautiful thought. I wonder if my mane and tail will bleach in the sun again this summer. My body hair usually gets a little lighter, but my mane and tail turn a lot lighter. And you know the white strip on my face? If I'm in the hot sun too long, it gets sunburned just like people. Sherry is the one who really gets it though. She's almost all white...and even her eyeballs seem to get sunburned. We'll stay in the regular barn during the heat of the day...and with the hayloft above us we should be cool and comfy.

Say Mother...is it true that Puddin was sold? To a lady who thinks he's a "king of the horse world?" Has Aunt Sugar heard from her wandering boy? Unless I'm a mile off-base, my Puddin-cousin will be contacting her often. He won't forget his mommie...or does he call her "mother" now?

How about Buggy? Is she still a home girl? Is Buggy small and dainty like Jezebel? I know Buggy got her pet name because Helen first called her "Little Lady Bug"...and her registered name is Galazal. But how on earth did Jezebel get her pet name? It sounds suspicious...ha! If I remember correctly, her registered name is Azal. She was very reserved, but Puddin and I had lots of fun with her young'un.

Remember when Puddin was gelded? Helen didn't want him running around with the gang until he was up to par again...so she put him in the paddock right next to our pasture. He was lonely in there...so she put me with him for company. That's when I learned to jump. If that fence between the paddock and the pasture is as high as it is in my mind's eye...Helen must have thought I had some jumping-bean-blood. Poor Puddin. And naughty Stick O'Candy! Every time Helen put me in the paddock with him, I'd be over the fence with you and the others as soon as she turned her back...and not even a year old, mind you! I should have had a good, sound spanking!

Chapter 9

Gracious sakes alive and dear me suzz!

You can scold me, Mother...for letting six whole months go by without one word from yours truly. Scold me thoroughly...so I won't have to have a guilty conscience. It isn't that I haven't thought of you every day...it's just that I haven't had a minute to sit down and concentrate.

To start with...there was my Horse Show. The very first one of my life. Then, there was Sherry's...but she's been in Shows before. And to top it all off...who should turn up at Candyhorse Farm but Jezebel. Has she always been so bossy, Mother? I don't remember her bossing me around so much when I was a little tyke there at Helen's. But gosh darn it...you'd think this was Jezebel Farm instead of Candyhorse...the way she tries to lay down the law to Sherry and me. What she needs is a good come-uppance if you ask me...to take the wind out of her sails.

About the Horse Show though...I didn't know there were that many horses in the whole wide world. And beautiful? Well just take a good look at daddy...then close your eyes and picture forty-seven more almost that elegant. I think forty-seven would be a very conservative estimate, and Mister does too. Maybe even forty-hundred.

The Horse Show was exciting...but we had a rough time going to and from it. Our new trailer for traveling is a big disappointment. It has a flapping roof. Mister says he should have his head examined for buying a homemade one instead of a store-bought. It was suppose to be sturdy and inexpensive...and it turned out to be wiggly and high-priced. The man who made it is a professional welder. He knew how to make the joints strong...but when it came to the roof...boy-oh-boy! It not only flaps...but Gulliver, himself, could stand in there without hunching down. There's plenty of space above my head when I stand up to put my front feet in the manger...and Mister says it's like pulling a silo down the road. They kept stopping on the side of the road to tie my neck-rope shorter...because they didn't want me putting my feet in the manger. Said if they had to stop fast...I'd wind up with my feet poking through the front of the trailer. I don't know how many times they stopped to shorten my rope...but by the time we reached the Horse Show I was practically in a straight jacket. When we came back home i was tied short right from the start.

Daddy was there, but I didn't get to see him. Saw Helen, though...she hugged me...and said, "Is this young lady my little tiny Sticky-girl?" I still love her very, very much. I didn't see daddy, but I heard enough about him. It was "Gabbar this" and "Gabbar that" all the time. The Horse Show barn was as long as your arm, and his stall was about a mile down the aisle. Missus said Honey better be careful or she'd wear a rut in the aisle running back and forth between our stalls. She kept spiriting his visitors up to my end of the barn...to see "Gabbar's daughter."

One man wants to buy me...but I wasn't worried. They couldn't have a Candyhorse Farm without a Candyhorse. Honey was worried though...and after the man went away

Stick O'Candy and Mister entering their first class.

she wanted to get a padlock for my door. Mister said, "Eh-oh, no...in case of fire in the barn, a padlocked stall might mean the difference between saving a horse and not saving it." So from then on, Honey parked herself on a stool outside my door...and when visitors came, she said very politely, "Candy isn't for sale...she's just here for the Show."

Gabbar (my daddy) was the "Grand Champion Stallion" of that Horse Show. And I won the third-place ribbon in the Halter Class. The judge was a man...and did he stare! He stared at me so much it made me squirm. Missus always tells Honey it isn't polite to stare at people...but I guess it's all right for judges to stare at horses. At a Horse Show, you're not suppose to act like a pet. You're not supposed to reach out and rub Mister's cheek with your nose the way you do at home. And you're not supposed to paw the ground and act like you're trying to dig a hole down to China. No matter how long the judge stands and stares at you, you're supposed to pretend you don't notice. You're supposed to stand with your feet square...like a box. And you're supposed to keep your ears pointed forward...even if you want to listen to noises behind you. Horse Shows have lots of rules and regulations.

Sherry and Honey in the costume made by Missus.

Sherry's Show must be exciting. Honey rode her with a fancy Indian Princess costume on. Missus made the whole outfit. Even a black velvet wig...with long, bumpity black braids. You can't see any of her own hair when she's wearing that wig. The dress is wine-color...with all colors of bead trim-ming...and white leather fringe around the bottom of the skirt. Missus can sew like a whizz...and the only time she needed any help was when all the fringe has to be cut. They all had callouses on their fingers from using the scissors so much. The skirt is so gathery-full that you can't tell from looking it's a "coulotte." In case you don't know...a "coulotte" is a "divided skirt, for riding horses." Honey wears soft white moc-casins...and a feather in her wig with that costume.

Missus made a big fur saddle-cover for Sherry to wear. She bought nine fox pelts from a man who makes fur coats for ladies. The pelts had been in cold storage for six years...and Missus got them for a dollar each. She said there were so many little legs dangling around Sherry's saddle-cover that the judge might think Honey was riding a centipede...ha! Sherry had fluffy Indian feathers on her head...and a "sun bonnet" of feathers on her tail.

She's such a dear old doll... that Sherry. She's bigger than Jezebel, but she just shrugs her shoulders when we get pushed around. I don't mean Jezebel actually pushes us around...but she's so darn fussy about everything. For instance when I'm eating a special patch of grass...she thinks she should have it. When they take us into the barn, she can't wait like a lady and take her turn...she has to be first. And when it's time to eat...she has to be first again. She's fussy like an old maid that wants her own way all the time...or like a spoiled child. Always wants to be in the middle of everything, too.

When it was just Sherry and me here at Candyhorse Farm, Honey could come out and practice me whenever she pleased. Sherry never tried to get in the middle of things. But Jezebel is so jealous for attention that she has to be put in the barn...and she raises a big stink unless Sherry's in there, too. Mister says Jezebel doesn't feel secure here yet. She just wants to be the big queen bee...that's what's the matter with her.

Chapter 10

Honestly, Mother!

Miz Prima Dona of Candyhorse Farm is really living it up. They don't call her Jezebel any more. Now her pet name is "Belle"...and that suits her just fine. She thinks she's the belle of the ball, and acts accordingly.

Mister hired a young college boy to work part-time out here, and he simply adores dear Belle. The other day he was in the aisle stirring up a week's supply of feed...and as he bent over one of the barrels, Belle stuck her head out and bit him on the croup. It startled him...but he thought it was funny. He even laughed when he told Mister about it! I didn't think it was anything to laugh at...he would have been hurt if it hadn't been for his tough trousers. He said Belle thought he wasn't moving fast enough...and it was her way to stop mixing and start feeding. Hope the belle of the ball starts feeling secure pretty soon...so things can get back to normal.

I'm in "basic training" for English, now, Mother. We started it early this summer with a "bitting rig." When you wear a bitting rig for the first time, you don't even know how to turn your head from one side to the other. You feel like you're all tied up in a bundle. You have a bridle on your head, a bit in your mouth, a girth around your middle, and a crupper under your tail. You have check reins and side reins coming from the girth...and attached to your bit and bridle. The bit has dingle-dangles on it to make you forget about the rest of the paraphernalia. The dingle-dangles are "toys'...to make you "bit-happy."

When they first put the bitting rig on, it's loose...and you don't think much about it. You start playing with those dingle-dangles, and they really are kind'a fun...you waller them around on your tongue. When you start actually enjoying it, they start tightening the reins about an inch at a time. You're so busy playing with the bit, that each time they take an inch off the reins, you adjust your chin and neck so you can still feel the dingle-dangles with your tongue. You don't wear the bitting rig very long at a time...because your neck gets tired. They don't run any risk of getting too much of an "arch" in it...they just want you to form the habit of holding your head proud, and tucking your chin in when you have a bit in your mouth.

As the reins get tighter (gradually, remember) you find out you're more comfortable if you "give" a little. If you didn't give a little, you'd be pulling at the bit...like a stubborn chin-sticker-outer. If you relax and enjoy yourself, it's easier to keep your balance and turn around and things. It's better to have people know what they're doing when they're using a bitting rig on a horse...if they go about it too fast, you're able to end up with a pitiful head-set instead of a proud, elegant head carriage. I was one that concentrated on my "toys" so seriously that learning the art of "giving to the bit" was no problem.

Jezebel arriving at the farm.

Everything hinges (or buckles) onto the girth around your middle...the reins, and the crupper, too. When you're not wearing the rig, it looks like a mad jumble of straps...and it hangs on the wall in the aisle. When it came from the factory in a box, it looked even worse...and you should have heard Missus go on when she unpacked it.

She said the crupper was a "breast collar for a midget work-horse"...the girth and body roller was a "contraption for a circus-horse"...the bit with dingle-dangles was a "gruesome weapon that would strangle a poor unsuspecting horse"...the bridle and short reins were "something someone dreamed up in a nightmare"...and she was all set to pack it right back to the factory by return mail. She kept her face straight, but of course she was just kidding...I think.

Three or four weeks later, when I felt perfectly at ease in the rig...they started me on "ground-driving." To do this, they used reins about twenty or thirty feet long. Instead of the short rein from the girth to my bit, they threaded the long reins through the girth (there's a ring on each side for this purpose) and attached one to each side of the bit. Then Honey went way back to the end of the reins, and Mister stayed up beside my head with a lead rope attached to my bridle. They had me outdoors for the ground-driving...out in the big pasture. Mister didn't lead me, or give me any directions...Honey did that from way out behind. When she wanted me to walk, she'd say, "Walk!"...and let the reins wiggle a little on my back.

We'd walk all over the pasture...loads of fun. To have me turn, she'd give a little tug, she'd tell Mister which way I was supposed to turn...he had to know that, so he wouldn't be putting any tension on the lead rope when I turned to the off side...and so he could stay out of my way when I turned toward him. They said, "An ounce of prevention is worth a pound of cure"...so Mister stayed with me with his lead rope for weeks and weeks. If you get excited and forget to follow directions coming from the long reins, you might get yourself all tangled up and frightened. You might even get so frightened you'd try to run away...and Honey would be flat on her face, dragging along behind.

They never did have me do any trotting at first...in fact they still don't. They think that part should wait until I'm pulling a cart with wheels on it. It's supposed to be "second nature" for me to "obey the commands" before we go on to the next step. Wish we still had that fancy sleigh with the red plush...but we gave it away when we moved from the half-acre, because the paint chipped off and the plush got raggy...from sitting out in the weather all the time. But heck! If Missus could upholster a saddle with fur, she could upholster a sleigh with plush...and a new coat of paint wouldn't be very hard to put on. We could have lots of fun in the snow this winter if we had that sleigh!

In the olden days people used to go jingling around in sleighs every winter. Sometimes the snow drifted so high they could ride right over the fences. Sometimes the horses would lose their footing and fall down in a jumble of tangled-up harness. The sleighs would tip over, and the people would scramble in the snow trying to find their Christmas packages. Honey says all the ladies wore beautiful velvet cloaks (red ones) trimmed with white fur...and the men wore powder in their wigs and britches. They didn't have anything but nuts and berries to eat and pot-bellied stoves. They had oil lamps and pumps to get their water out of. Honey knows all kinds of things about olden days. Her Dinpop is where she learns all the stuff.

Chapter 11

Groundhog Day again!

And if I remember correctly, it was before Thanksgiving when I talked to you last. The older I get, the faster time flies. I'm officially four years old now...and it won't be long before I'm really four.

Speaking of Thanksgiving...I'm thankful that I never got into a knock-down-drag-out with Belle when she was being so bossy. Know why? She's going to have a baby! Poor girl...she's almost as big as the barn. This has been a really tough winter...still is...and it's been hard for her to get around outdoors in the snow. Sherry and I are able to get all the exercise we want...but poor Belle has all she can do to stay on her feet.

Mister and Honey practically hold their breath when she goes in and out the door of the barn. If she ever slipped...no telling what would happen. The floors of our stalls have thick wooden planks over the cement but the aisle is just plain bare cement. They put sawdust and straw in the aisle to help Belle keep her balance. The sawdust and straw are for Sherry and me, too...on account of the chunks of ice that form on horses' hooves in cold, snowy weather.

Your feet can be absolutely clean and dry when you go out of the barn, but they don't stay that way. After while you feel like you're walking around with icebergs on the bottom of each foot. It has something to do with the heat of your body. Your hooves are senseless...I mean the don't have any feeling...and they don't need heat. They get just as cold as ice, but it doesn't bother them a bit. Inside the hoof ring is you...and you do have heat...they call the part of your hoof that has the body heat the "frog."

You get out of the barn with your feet warm and dry all over. As you walk around in the snow, it begins to pack up in there between your hoof and your frog. Your frog is trying to stay warm, and your hoof gradually cools down to the temperature of the snow...and then the trouble begins. The tightly-packed snow turns to ice...and poor little "froggy" loses the battle. Pretty soon you have ice caked all over the bottom of all four feet, and one time I was a whole inch taller than normal when I came in from outside. They have us go through the barn door slowly in the summer...and even more slowly in the winter. Ice packs are dangerous enough for horses not in foal...think how risky they would be for pregnant ones. Golly...if Belle ever slipped and fell...I don't want to even think about what might happen.

I like her now, Mother. Sherry and I both do. She has such dainty manure, and she's an exceptionally fine specimen...Mister says. She's a Polish Arabian...with a "dam" named Fa Gazal (that's her mother)...and a sire named Azrak (her father)...and Belle's registered name is Azal. Belle is married to Gabbar...so her baby will be either my half-sister or my half-brother. I still can't understand why daddy can have so many wives. Mister can only have one...Missus. Honey doesn't have any brothers or sisters, and I must have forty-seven at least...wouldn't you say?

Honey with her best friend and playmate, Sally-dog.

Another thing about Belle...she's a "good house-keeper"...and she has a "bathroom" in her stall to keep her manure in. Our college boy just loves to clean her stall because she goes to the bathroom in the corner of her stall to put her manure in all the time, and he doesn't have to hunt for it. He says Belle's manure is just as little and dainty as Belle, herself...and he thinks it's because she's a Polish Arabian...is that so? He says he could carry out her manure in a teacup. If that's really true, I think Belle must be constipated. The veterinarian should come out and stick a tube up her nose, because she probably has the colic and doesn't realize it.

I had colic once and believe you-me, I knew it. Sicker than anything, I was. We were living by the Country Club then...before we moved and got Sherry. It came on so fast. I was perfectly okay one minute, and all of a sudden I was anything but okay. Honey was bringing milk out to Stuffy and her kittens...and found me groaning my head off. She went screaming to the house, and Mister and Missus came running out. He grabbed my halter and took me outdoors. Missus ran to call the veterinarian, and Honey kept saying, "Will she be all right, Daddy? Will Candy be all right?" Mister said, "We have to keep her walking, Honey...that's the only thing I know." Round and round the paddock we went. With me as weak as a kitten, and him saying,

"Come on, Candy-girl...don't lie down on me." When the veterinarian came, he said, "Not good! Not good! Keep her walking while I get this thing ready!"

"This thing" was a long rubber tube. He stuck it in one of my nostrils and pushed it in so far I thought it would go right on through and out the other end. It didn't, though. He poured some medicine through the tube so it could reach "the trouble spot" right now. He said the medicine was supposed to go to work and save my life. Colic is a terrible thing for horses. They walked me again. When the veterinarian left, he said to walk me until after my "bowels had moved." We walked and walked...first Mister leading me and then Honey taking a turn. They put a blanket over me and Missus brought warm coats out for my leaders. They took me up by the house so the electric light could shine on me...because they didn't want to miss it if my bowels did move.

If I hadn't been so miserable, it would have been funny. Missus kept sticking her head out the door...saying, "Any manure yet?" And when there was some manure you would have thought it was Christmas and groundhog Day and the Fourth of July all rolled up together. I began to feel better right away but we kept walking for probably a hundred miles...they didn't take any chance of letting me lie down too soon. By the time they took me back to my barn, it was getting daylight...and I felt like a million dollars.

Lordy I hope Belle doesn't get the constipated colic with that baby coming a long. I can hardly wait to see the little dickens. Wonder whether it will be a boy or a girl. We're trying to think up a good name for it. Sometime for Arabian foals they invent a name by using part of the dam's name and part of the sire's name...and we've thought of some real dandies. For Azal and Gabbar it could be Gabaz, Gabzal, Azgab, Azalbar, Zalgab...dozens of high-sounding names. We could say it was the name of some Polish king or something that owned one of Belle's ancestors. Polish is what Honey puts on her boots to keep the leather nice.

Hey! Something's up! All of a sudden the whole family is out here polishing me. Shining me up within an inch of my life. A Horse Show at this time of year? On Groundhog Day? I wonder what on earth!

Chapter 12

Something was up, all right, all right!

Listen, my mother, and you shall hear
of the midnight ride of your daughter dear.
On the day after Groundhog Day, fifty-seven,
what rhymes with that, dearie,
nothing but heaven,

So I'll stop playing with poetry, and tell you what happened. By the time they tucked me in bed that night, the cat was out of the bag. The very next night I had a ride that did last until midnight...until after midnight, to be exact. I was taken to a professional horse trainer...and this is the first time I've had a chance to relax for about seven or eight minutes.

It was a "lady" horse trainer...but don't think I had it soft! I had to sit up and tend to my knittin' every minute I was there. That's a new expression I learned...an expression I couldn't help but learn, you might say. All the time, it was "Candy! Tend to your knittin' or I'll give you a taste of you-know -what!" "You-know-what" was a little brown leather bat with fringe on one end. I really like the taste of leather...but something in the tone of her voice made me think her leather fringe had something icky on it. Rancid oil, maybe.

She said my "basic training" made me easy to work with. Before you could say "Jack Robinson" I was pulling a cart...and she was riding me all over the place. I already knew what the words "walk" and "trot" meant...and she taught me some silent signals that mean the same words. You learn to feel the words instead of hearing them. I already knew what "back" meant...and there's a silent signal for that word, too. The only word I hadn't already learned was "canter," so I had to learn the spoken word and the silent signal at the same time. Easy, though...cantering is just like galloping, only you go a lot slower. A good trainer can teach you walk, trot, canter, and whoa "on command"...without getting you all confused.

First she rode me inside the fence...in the "training ring"...even in the snow, mind you. When the snow as all gone, we went out on the country roads...roads with bridges sometimes. All the bridges were made out of heavy wooden planks...but they didn't sound the same as the planks on our stall floors. They sounded hollow and clippity-clop. The bridges had water under them, and if you looked down you could see it between the planks. Sometimes I felt like refusing to step foot on a bridge...even after I knew I wasn't going to fall through...then she's remind me of that you-know-what, and how bad it would taste. It's better to go across a bridge without looking down at the water...then you won't get dizzy.

Honey and Candy at the her first show under saddle.

Honey came up to stay with me after I'd been in training for about three months. My lady-trainer said, "I've ridden the daylights out of your Candyhorse, and now you can take over." Honey was just like a kid with a new toy. She just couldn't get over the idea of being able to ride on my back...I'm still "just a baby" to the family. At first, she rode me inside the fence...while she learned my signals. Then we went out on the roads and had long practice-sessions every day. Once, Honey asked if it would be okay to ride me into the town...and my trainer said "Sure! Just be careful not to run over the pedestrians."

Everything was fine and dandy. That is, everything was fine and dandy until we reached the longest bridge you ever saw in your life! Talk about water! There was a regular ocean under that bridge...and it wasn't made out of planks...it was solid cement! Even if it had the same kind of railings, I was very suspicious when it didn't have that hollow, clippity-clop sound. Your darling daughter decided not to risk it...and Honey doesn't use that leather bat with the fringe, so she was stymied for a minute. I didn't pay any heed to walk, trot or canter...and I knew she wouldn't expect me to go across the bridge if she tried whoa...so I was ready to turn around and go back when rat-a-tat-tat! A pair of heels beat a tattoo on my sides and I was so surprised I was halfway across the river before I knew what was happening. She slowed me down to a walk and said, "That's right, young lady! I said we were going to town...and to town we go!"

We went back and forth across that bridge...and I got so used to it I could have crossed it in my sleep. Honey praised me a lot...and kept telling me I was a good girl...we really had a good time that day. I can understand almost everything she says...just by the tone of her voice.

We went to several small Horse Shows with the trainer...and then came the big Arabian Horse Show. I won first in my Halter Class, and when Honey rode me in the English Pleasure Class, we won third. The big Show was held outdoors...on a very, very windy day. In the morning during the Halter Classes it was blowing a real gale...scraps of paper and dust were flying all over the place, and the other horses were excited and jumpy. The judge practically stared a hole through me, and he startled Honey when he said, "You sure you're in the right class with this filly? Looks like a purebred." He didn't crack a smile, and Honey got all tangled up...saying, "No sir...I mean yes sir...we're in the right class. She's three-fourths Arabian."

That judge was nice. He patted me...or maybe he was feeling my withers, because judges do feel them sometimes. When they announced over the loudspeaker...first place, Stick O'Candy of Candyhorse Farm, Honey looked me in the face and said, "Candy...that's you!" She acted like she expected me to go after the blue ribbon and the trophy all by myself...boy, it was exciting.

In the afternoon during the Performance Classes the wind wasn't blowing quite so hard, thank goodness. before the English Pleasure Class Mister had Honey ride me in the open, so he could take some pictures. She wore a brown derby hat, a white riding coat, brown Kentucky jodhpurs (pants), a white shirt with a regular necktie, and brown leather jodhpur boots. I wore my English saddle and bridle, period.

Belle had foaled little Ibn Gabbar about a week before Honey had come up to the trainer's place, and she was excited about getting back home to see him. Ibn Gabbar...son of Gabbar...and half-brother of Stick O'Candy. The night he was foaled was a wild one, and not on account of the weather! There's a lot to tell about it, but do you mind if I go to sleep now...and finish this early in the morning? I'm one tired Candyhorse!

Chapter 13

Fresh as a daisy and raring to go.

But before I pick up where I left off last night, let me tell you this little half-brother of mine is the cutest thing you ever laid eyes on. He's having his before-breakfast snack right now...and does he love his milk. Slurp...slurp...slurp. He thinks he and his mommie are all alone now...doesn't remember he's in a barn with two other grown-ups. Sherry and I get the biggest kick out of peeking through the boards and keeping track of his goings-on.

The little pot really orders Belle around...gets by with murder, if you ask me...figuratively speaking, of course. What gets me is that he's so innocent about everything. Sometimes when he's nursing, he bangs so hard it even hurts me...but Belle just stands there patiently and puts up with it. He really isn't trying to hurt...it's just his way of saying, "Mommie! I'm hungry! Let down your milk?" He had the most loving mommie a little hor-sie could have...but I guess she wasn't very loving the night he was foaled.

The night Ibby arrived, Belle didn't want him...she didn't want to have anything to do with him. A foal needs his mother's new milk right away...it was colostrum in it to start the bowels working, and it has kind of a medi-cine in it to help the baby stay healthy. But Belle did her level best to keep him far, far away...acted like a holy terror, I guess. They phoned Helen, and she came to the rescue...with her husband and her sister-in-law. It took five people working together to get that baby his first drink of milk.

I guess Honey and the sister-in-law were steering him to the nipple all the time...and Mister, Helen and her husband were trying to make Belle stand still. she's start pushing him away again. Ibby must have been pretty strong and healthy to begin with, because it took them over two hours to convince Belle that she should let him have a drink. The funny part of it is that the minute she did let him nurse, she turned into a good mother imme-diately. And acted like she was saying, "What's all the fuss about?" So after the baby had his first bowel movement...on Honey's boots, incidental-ly...they all went in the house for a night-time snack. I guess the morning sun was shining when "the first aid crew" left for home...and both the "patients" were doing fine.

I'm sorry I wasn't here that night. I'd give my shirt to hear Helen calling me her "Sticky-girl" again...music to my ears the way she used to say it. When

Helen talked to me it was like getting my hair stroked gently. Does her voice make you feel like that? Nuzzle her cheek for me, will you?

She'd love to watch the show our baby boy puts on every morning when we first go outdoors. He runs big circles around us...then smaller circles...and the circles keep getting smaller, until he can dash past somebody's tail...and grab a hair inside his mouth without slowing down. After he grabs himself a hair, he takes off lickety-split in the most convenient direction. He seems to have a preference for white hairs...and Sherry pretends she doesn't notice when he makes off with one. He plays that game about three times...and then the green grass attracts his attention.

If you want a good chuckle, just watch a young foal trying to reach his nose down far enough to eat grass. He has to spend his legs apart, bend his knees...go through all kinds of contortions before he gets one little nibble. Then, chances are that he won't know how to chew it after he get it. Ibby

Mister, Honey and Wendy.

sees us grown-ups grazing...so he thinks he should, too.

He's like that with his mother in their stall. He has his own private grain bucket, but he likes to eat out of hers. Belle is tied by her own serving of grain...so she doesn't get a chance at his until he's had all he wants to eat. He takes turns with his bites...one from mommie's, one from his own, one from hers, another from him. He's such a busy little body...and so handsome! Just wait until an Arabian judge gets a look at him. The new veterinary thinks he's perfect, the family thinks he's perfect, both Sherry and I think he's perfect...and whoever thinks we're prejudiced has another thing coming. Ha!

When Honey and I came home from training there was a wonderful surprise waiting for us. A large, oval, riding ring with a wooden fence around it. Mister and Missus had done all of the work themselves...without mentioning it to Honey. And was she tickled. They had it painted yellow and brown to match the house...with a wide dirt track just outside the fence, and grass left to grow inside the track. Right in the middle, there's an electric light on a tall pole. Honey practices Sherry and me on the track every day...sometimes again in the evening. We'll be able to use the ring when the days are short, too. Just turn on the electric light, and away we go. If the snow gets as high as the fence...over we'll go. I think.

Well...we had Ibby this summer, and next summer we're going to have a bunch of funny little Collie puppy dogs! A lady gave Prinka's full sister to us...but with dogs, full sisters are called "litter sisters." Prinka is tricolor...black, white, and tan. And her sister, Wendy, is a sable...which is goldy-tan, trimmed with white around her neck. She'll be bred to a fancy male Collie in the spring...and before you know it, we'll have a pile of puppies. Honey will probably carry them around in a doll blanket like she did Prinka.

She'd have a heck of a time carrying Prinka around in her arms now. That dog is huge, and so is Wendy. Sally-dog is the tiny one now...but she rules the roost, you can bet on that. Mister says the young ones "respect her middle-aged dignity." She's practically human, you know. She's a mind reader. She was six months old when they got her, and the only thing they had to do to get her trained was read a book about training dogs. All of a sudden she knew what to do and when to do it. Wendy and Prinka are both smart enough...but they're so bouncy. Missus says they have to be toned down somehow or the house will fall apart. I guess they go leaping around like a pair of bulls in a china closet, and nothing, but nothing is sacred. Honey says they think they're just cuddly little lap dogs. Lap dogs! Whoosh! Lap dogs for Gulliver, maybe.

It's a marvel to me that Gray Stuffy doesn't get herself hurt the way she gets right in the middle of those two. Maybe they respected her middle-aged dignity, too. But we don't even know how old she is.

Chapter 14

Over the river and through the woods!

That's a song for Thanksgiving Day. Everyone in the house is having turkey with dressing...and everyone in the barn is having a feast for "drinkers of the wind." Did you know Arabian horses are "drinkers of the wind?" It's because they have such large nostrils and windpipes. In the Bible, where they have The Ten Commandments for people, they have a beautiful part about Arabian horses. It goes:

The glory of his nostrils is terrible.
He paweth in the valley, and rejoiceth in his
strength;
He goeth on to meet the armed men.
He mocketh at fear and is not affrighted:
neither turneth he back from the sword.
The quiver rattleth against him, the glittering spear
and the shield.
He swalloweth the ground with fierceness and rage:
neither believeth he that it is the sound of the
trumpet.
He saith among the trumpets, ha ha; and he
smelleth the battle afar off,
the thunder of the captains, and the shouting.

They say Arabians have good width between the jaws, for their large windpipes. And extra spring of the ribs, so they can have big lung capacity. With so much fresh air, their blood can oxidize just right...and their muscles don't get tired.

There are lots of legends about Arabian horses...and they say it's hard to know which are true, and which grew out of sentimental imagination. They were war horses on the desert in olden times, and the legends about them are all very fascinating. The chiefs and their tribes didn't have anything but horses for transportation..and they did a lot of traveling, so they had to know quite a bit about their trusty steeds. They were always fighting with other chiefs and tribes, too...and it stands to reason that whatever chief knew the most about horses would probably win all the "skirmishes." Skirmishes are battles. The really smart chiefs always told their men to keep an eye on the enemies' horses. If the enemies had white horses in the lead, they were supposed to tempt them into fighting on the sunny side of the hill. That legend sounds logical...Sherry is white, and the sun really bothers her.

We don't have any black horses so I don't know whether the legend about them is logical or not. Anyway...if an enemy had black horses in the lead, the smart chiefs tried to steer the fighting onto rocky ground. The blacks are supposed to be afraid of rocky ground. Maybe they had tender frogs, or something.

Sherry and Honey out for a ride.

I'm a chestnut, and just listen to this! The chestnuts and bays were supposed to be the toughest to beat of all. And they could run fastest. If a chief and his tribe were riding chestnuts and bays, themselves... and came up against another tribe with chestnuts and bays...they figured they could stick it out because the battle would be even-steven. But a chief who didn't have chestnuts and bays to go against them with, would gather up his tribe and get the heck out of there. They'd have to run like sixty, too...but the chestnuts and bays would probably catch them anyway. Chestnuts would even fly into the air during a big fight...they weren't afraid of anything...and they were very, very valuable.

The bays were thought to be the hardiest of all...and the most sober. On top of being able to run the legs off most horses, they could leap down to the bottom of a precipice without having to scramble to keep their balance. They could leap straight down, without getting hurt. I can leap up and over, but I never tried leaping straight down...we don't have any precipices to practice on.

Belle was black when she was foaled...did you know that? Now she's dark gray, with quite a bit of black in her mane and tail. I don't know whether or not she would be afraid of rocky ground...and I don't know whether her frogs are more tender than Sherry's and mine or not, either. That legend about the blacks sounds a little far-fetched to me, anyway.

Another thing the Arabs said about horses...was if a horse could reach down and drink from a stream that was level with the ground, without bending its knees...then that horse had perfect conformation. I don't know what they said about the little foals...or maybe foals in those days had longer necks and shorter legs. Ibby is a chestnut like me...and he really lives up to the legend. When he runs in his big circles he goes with the speed of light...and when he feels especially kippy, he flies so high you'd think he had wings.

We had a terrible fright the other day, with Ibby. He was running around and having fun like he always does, and ran right into a woven wire fence. The fence was new...and temporary. They had put it up to keep us away from a gate they were building at the corner of the big pasture. Ibby didn't even see it until the last moment...and then he tried to rear up and back from it. His hind feet slipped out from under him and one foot got caught in the wires. He fell on his back, and lay very still. Belle saw it happen and went flying to his rescue...but he was caught by the wire, and there wasn't anything she could do. He didn't even try to move.

Belle began to scream. She stood right over him...screaming and screaming. The wind was blowing hard, and with the house windows shut, the family didn't hear her calling for help until they just happened to step out the door for something. They came on the run, and when they saw Ibby caught in the fence, Missus took a detour for the wire cutters. They got him loose, and the only thing he had was a little scratch on his pastern. They looked all over him carefully, put medicine on his scratch...and soothed both of them for a while. Ibby was dancing around and feeling fine in just a few minutes.

It was almost as if Belle was thanking them for saving her baby. She had screamed so...and with him lying still, it looked like he was unconscious. I do think he must have been stunned for awhile. I never want to see a sight like that again in my whole life. We love that little boy-doll. Mr. Mischief of nineteen-fifty-seven. Friends of the family are always coming to take a look at him...they say there's something special about him, namely...perfection.

I could go on and on, Mother...but we're going out to the riding ring. Honey's taking me English, and Mister's taking Sherry Western. We'll have a little performance Class all our own...with Missus for the audience, plus Sally, Prinka, Wendy, Gray Stuff, and whoever else happen along.

Chapter 15

Dasher, Dancer, Prancer, Vixen...Comet, Cupid, Donner, Blitzen!

And tonight's the night! It's a tradition in my family to put out a little snack for Santa...something to warm up his innards. When she was little, Honey always put some fruitcake and milk on the dining room table...and now she takes Mister's advice and puts out a glass of "snort." Honey still prefers the fruitcake and milk idea, but Mister says Santa is a man...nothing warms a man's innards as well as a little snort.

Milk is cold, and snort is warm. It's plenty cold tonight, that's for sure...wouldn't mind having a little snort myself. I think it must be colder now than it was this afternoon when we were outdoors. You should have seen the ice packs on our feet...and we were only out about one hour. It was four below zero then, with the sun shining. Now that it's dark, it must be eighty below...or even twenty.

They really have to hang onto Ibby when they lead him into the barn...the little pot wants to play all the time, not just part of the time. He doesn't care how much he slides around...not that little minx. He's started the cutest little baby habit, now. When he turns his head around now, he bobs it...so innocent and sweet. He does it when he eats his grain, too. Mother, he's gorgeous! Perky little pointed ears, and always turning them in every direction trying to hear everything that goes on. Big dark eyes, a teen-sy-weensy muzzle, a smooth little dish in his pretty face. Of course you know I don't mean a dish like people eat picnic dinners on...I mean the con-cave shape below the eyes, like Gabbar and Belle have.

He's a good little eater, too...has powdered milk mixed with his feed, and gobble, gobble, gobble...he doesn't miss his mommie's milk at all. He's growing, naturally, but because we're with him all the time, he still seems just a tiny baby.

Say, I've been trying to remember to tell you about Wendy and Prinka. You wouldn't recognize them now...they're so ladylike. They've been to dog school. Night Dog School. Mister and Honey went too. They had a course on dog obedience at the local high school, and Missus said, "That's for us!" It worked, too. I've watched them practice...they bring the dogs out to the big pasture, and I have a ringside seat here at my window. Doesn't matter how cold it is, or how snowy...Mister works with Prinka, and Honey with Wendy.

Dogs are supposed to do the same things horses do, but they use different words. The way they talk about it, there were all kinds of dogs at that school. Each dog had a handler...pets and owners, like our four. No private lessons...and will wonders never cease, no dog fights. They had one Toy Pomeranian that our collie could have swallowed without chewing, a couple of Police dogs (German Shepards), several Dukes Mixtures, some Spaniels, and Mister said they all graduated with flying colors.

At the first lesson, the instructor said the handlers would have to talk to their dogs with a tone of command in their voices, no matter how much they loved them. Mister used the tone of command right away, but Honey didn't want to...thought it would hurt the dogs' feelings. She learned she had to do it, though, to make her dog take her seriously. Another thing that sounds cruel, but isn't cruel if used properly, is the choke chain. This chain is attached to the end of a short leather leash, and is looped around the dog's neck. The dog first learns to "heel"...at the left side of the handler. It's supposed to travel just as fast as the handler, and keep its head in line with the handler's body. If it goes too fast, the person jerks on the leash and says, "Prinka, Heel!" This reminds the dog to tend to her knittin'...and the same thing happens if the dog lags behind. It's surprising how soon our dogs pop to attention when they hear the commands. "Wendy, Heel!" "Prinka, Heel!" The dogs don't like it when the chain jerks...they prefer to obey the oral command and that's why it's important to make a command really sound like one. It's actually a kindness in the long run.

At the second lesson they learned "Prinka, Sit!"..."Wendy, Sit!" Then they combined the two commands, and when the handler has the dog heeling along in good style, he was supposed to stop and the dog had to sit immediately. They said all the dogs in class caught on right away, and hardly anyone had to jerk the leash more than once or twice. Missus had watched the lessons and she could make it work with both our dogs, too.

I think the third lesson covered sit, stay, and down, stay...the fourth covered sit, stay, come, sit and down, stay, come, down...the fifth was a real challenge. They said that fifth lesson separated the men from the boys, and I should think it would! The dogs had to sit, stay while their handlers went out of sight! The little Pomeranian practically lost it's mind when the lady tried to go away, and she wouldn't even attempt it for fear one of the big dogs would eat her little darling . A chubby little Duke's Mixture went waddling after the child it loved. One of the Spaniels howled like a banshee. Prinka stayed in a sitting position, but kept scooching her fanny along the floor in the direction Mister was trying to go. And Wendy! They said Wendy sat there cool as a cucumber and let Honey go way out of the gymnasium. Mister said she stayed there because he had to keep starting over with

Prinka, and whenever he said sit, stay...Wendy thought he was talking to her. Ha!

The sixth lesson was the last one, and it consisted of a run-down on everything they had learned, plus a graduation ceremony, plus refreshments and fun in general. My family met a lot of nice, nice people, and even though they have learned how to give this much training to dogs...they want to take the course again in the future, because genuine dog-lovers are fun to get acquainted with.

There is a terrific difference in people, Mother...some people can't stand animals of any kind. Missus says they miss out on a lot of happiness. She says it's the woman of the house that gives, or refuses to give this happiness to her husband and children. Her mother wasn't a horsewoman, but she was definitely a lover of animals. Long, long ago...their little dog named Fido got a broken leg. Her mother made a splint, and the leg was as good as new a few weeks later. Before the miracle drugs were discovered, their little Pekinese named Bebe came down with a deadly case of distemper. The veterinarian said there was no hope but her mother said, "Give me what medicine you have...I'll take care of her." And she did! Bebe was loved back to perfect health.

She mentioned other pets in her family...I'll tell you more, sometime.

Chapter 16

Mother...Ibby is dead.

I haven't been able to tell you before. Little Ibby is dead and we don't have him any more. The extra stall they built for him has been taken apart and the feed barrels are there again. The aisle in front of our stalls is just an aisle...our baby isn't dancing back and forth in it now. The boards for his floor have been taken up...nothing but cement there...nothing but feed barrels and cement where Ibby used to be. He was so beautiful, Mother. He was so good. So dear to Candyhorse Farm. It's awfully quiet...without Ibby.

There wasn't anything wrong with him, Mother. He was strong...and healthy. In January, the man came to trim our hooves...an old man. He's been around horses all his life, and he looked at Ibby and said, "I hate to be the one to tell you, but I think he's sick." He said Ibby didn't have a normal reaction when he put his hand near his eyes. He said the way he bobbed his little head wasn't a baby trait...it meant something was going wrong.

We called the veterinarian, and when he looked at Ibby he said there couldn't be anything very serious the matter...he was in such top condition. We waited a while and then called another veterinary from another city. He said Ibby's reactions to sudden movements of his hands around his head and eyes didn't seem typical of a healthy colt, but he didn't know... Old horsemen came to see Ibby, and one said our little fellow acted like a colt that had been struck by lightening. We hadn't had any electrical storms during Ibby's life.

Ibby kept on eating...never had a temperature...but he began to fall down. At first he'd just fall once. Then he'd fall once, then fall again when he was trying to get back up. He'd be perfectly all right, then maybe two times a day he'd lose his balance and fall down. In between those times, he'd be his own cute little self...and he even seemed to be better lots of days. None of the veterinarians we called to Candyhorse Farm recognized the symptoms...so we decided to take him to the Large Animal Clinic at the State Agricultural College. Mister tightened the roof on the trailer. He tied bales of straw along the walls, and padded the straw with blankets. One night he backed the trailer to the door of the barn...they were going to take Ibby to the hospital the next morning.

He went into Ibby's stall to try his halter on to see if it was a good fit...and Ibby fell down. He tried to get up, and fell down again. He became frantic and try as he would...he couldn't get up on his feet. Mister was helpless...he couldn't help. Ibby was big and strong, and Mister couldn't hold him. He fell, and he fell, hurting himself on the walls. Finally he fell, and lay still. Mister ran to the house to do the only thing there was to do...phone for the veterinarian.

The veterinarian came and was hard and short-tempered. How I wish my own doctor had been here at that time...he moved away two years ago. Ibby was badly hurt...beyond hope...but he was alive. And the man snarled at Mister for calling him out in the middle of the night on a hopeless case. Mister wishes now he had ordered him to leave and never come back. He wishes he had called a real friend to come and help with what had to be done. But he'd never had any experience before...no experience that taught him how to put a little baby horse to sleep.

He says now that anything would have been kinder than the way it was done. While he sat on the floor of the stall holding Ibby's poor little head on his lap, the veterinary stormed out to go back to his office for what he needed. He came back and gave Ibby a shot...Ibby didn't die. He gave him another shot...and Ibby didn't go to sleep. Mister pled with him to use something stronger, and the man said, "The shots I gave him should have killed ten horses!" He said if he had to go back and mix something stronger it would take two hours...and Mister said, "Go!" Mister sat there holding Ibby...and the man came back later. He gave Ibby and new shot and Mr. Mischief went away.

The veterinarian apologized. He said he couldn't stand to see animals suffer. He said sometimes mortally wounded animals have abnormal powers...but he hadn't dreamed it would take the stronger potion for a colt so young. He said the first shot should have put Ibby to sleep. Mister said, "You're right, doctor...the first shot should have put Ibby to sleep." His cheek muscles were working as he walked out of Ibby's stall. He opened the barn door, and his face was expressionless as he said again, "You're right, doctor...one shot should have been enough. Your work here is finished now. Good night, sir." And the man looked down as he went out of our barn for the last time.

That's the way it happened, Mother. I'm through talking about it now. But I'll never stop wishing Ibby's story could have been happy all the way. I wish you had known him like I did. I can close my eyes now and see him sticking his nodey down to the water in the tank...and being surprised to find it cold and wet. Frolicking about...learning how to reach down far enough to graze like the grown-ups...racing like the wind...his little tail carried high like a flag. Such a happy boy...my baby brother, he was, but you already knew that.

A man looked at me the other day and said, "A beautiful mare like that should be producing. She looks more like a perfect purebred than some of the purebreds do!" Missus said, "Maybe sometime. She's almost five now, but she's still our little Candyhorse. She can wait...we like her just the way she is." I don't feel much like a grown-up mare. I feel like a big baby...and I'm glad they like me just the way I am. This summer Honey will ride me every day, and Sherry, too. We'll be out in the ring and have a good ole' time. Sometimes we'll have it like a Horse Show...we did it last summer lots of time. We'll have it just like it was last summer. Missus will sit on the fence and be the audience.

And this summer we'll have some furry Collie puppy dogs playing around the place. Wendy will be the mommie. Honey will carry the puppies around in doll blankets with just their little nodeys sticking out...a whole pile of puppies in doll blankets...with bright little shoe-button eyes. We'll have lots of fun around this place...you just wait and see.

I guess I'll stop for now, Mother. Honey just came into the barn with our college boy, and they'll go into Belle's stall to pet her. They always do...and I love to watch them brush her till she shines like a mirror. Our college boy loves Belle very much. He has bright red hair and freckles. His mother died when he was a little fellow. He loves Belle and Wendy...and they love him.

Chapter 17

Auntie Prinka the Baby Sitter!

Wendy turned her puppies over to Prinka right after they were weaned...and good riddance! Prinka could hardly wait to start playing with them, and Wendy would hardly wait to see the last of the little monsters with their sharp, pointed teeth. She fussed over them like a mother hen for the first week, relaxed and enjoyed them for the next three weeks, barely put up with them during the last two weeks of nursing...and Prinka's been their boss-lady ever since.

Speaking of mother hens! Honey couldn't sit still for a minute the day the puppies arrived. It was the fifth of July when Wendy showed signs of whelping. Nine o'clock in the morning, just Wendy, alone...by two o'clock in the afternoon it was Wendy, plus eight little squirmers that didn't look any more like Collie dogs than the man in the moon. Honey was sure they were Duke's Mixtures, and they had guarded Wendy so carefully she wondered how it could possibly have happened. Duke's Mixtures or not...they belonged to Candyhorse Farm, and the first one to say they were less than perfect would have an argument on his hands.

That whelping business was entirely new to Wendy..she didn't know what was happening. Something made her strain like fury, and out popped a little still-born thing. She strained again, and out popped a live one. She licked the daylights out of it, and chewed the navel cord too short. While she was straining to have the third one, Honey doctored the over-licked puppy...but couldn't save it. From then on, they came too fast to get over-licked, and Honey had to help dry them off. Imagine having seven hungry mouths to feed. All at the same time!

Everyone was relieved when the production line shut down...especially my dear friend, Honey. She watched like a hawk to see that each baby had a nipple plugged in every few minutes...you know how important that colostrum in new-mother's-milk is. When the babies fell asleep, she'd put them in a safe pile so Wendy could have room to rest. They became so active that in spite of all the care, one of them scrambled around behind Wendy and got smothered between her and the wall. After that happened, they put a guard-rail around the walls...just high enough off the floor to keep a clear passage around mama when she lay down. From then on, everything was hunky-dory. Once in a while they would bring the little furballs out on the grass...for "exercise."

Did I ever tell you about the doghouse, here? They fixed it up early this summer. To get away from the constant worry about the dogs getting out on the road in front of a car, they had already fenced a large area between the riding ring and the house . There aren't any trees there for protection against the hot sun, so they dragged a tiny barn in the dogyard. Too tiny for even one horse, but huge compared to the average doghouse. I should think about fifteen full-grown Scotch Collies could lie down in there without being crowded. They insulated it, then put smooth boards on the inside walls. It has a door for people, a small door for dogs to run in and out of, and two glass windows they can open and shut. They put strong, woven wire over the windows so strange dogs can't get at Wendy when she was in season. No strange dogs ever came around our place, though...and incidentally, there wasn't any reason to worry about her puppies being Duke's Mixtures. When they began to grow, their heads began to lengthen out...they're purebreds, but had stubby little noses at first.

Anyway...Sherry and Belle and I had lots of sideshows to watch as we ate the grass in the middle of the track. While Wendy was nursing babies, Sally and Prinka couldn't use the dogyard...so they'd hang around with us horses and watch through the fence. Sally was mildly curious, but Prinka just ached to get in and get acquainted. Sally and Prinka are spayed...so they won't ever be mama-dogs.

Pablum is what to feed young puppies. Pablum and Milk in a glass pie pan. They'd walk right into their Pablum. They'd even go to sleep in it. Missus had to run after the camera once, to take a picture of the way they were all sleeping. Two in the Pablum, one half in and half out, one draped over the empty red milk glass, and two snuggled up to the Pablum box. The pictures is in color, and the puppies look like gold in the grass. It took them awhile to acquire a real taste for nourishment other than Wendy's milk, but by the time they were weaned, they were gobbling out of a great big cake pan.

After Auntie Prinka took over it was a regular circus...with her so smug and pleased you would have thought they were her own children. No matter where they were, she kept an eye on them. Good ole Sally-dog would lie in the sunshine, out of harm's way...Wendy would be out in the horse barn, or scouting around in the pasture...and Prinka never got tired of her baby-sitting job. She'd let them use her for a trampoline...they'd snuggle up and sleep with her...and she passed out discipline without playing favorites. Once in awhile the play got too rough, and she'd tone it down in short order.

The first time she had to get tough with them, the family came running. Two of the puppies had started a real dog fight, and in order to stop it, she had to get one of them down, and scare the other one away. The noise was terrible, and when the family saw her growling over a "little helpless puppy" they were all set to give her the dickens. Just about that time, the puppies got out of the fighting mood, and Prinka let them get back together again. Mister was ready to give Prinka a hard scolding, when some sixth sense made Missus say, "Don't! The puppy isn't hurt...and we don't know how it started." They've been glad a hundred times since then that they didn't punish her...because, watching closely, they discovered that the only time Prinka acted tough with those puppies was when they started a fight, and she was putting a stop to it.

One little fellow was a regular "personality boy" right from the start. The way he'd sit on one hip and cock his head to one side as he looked up to your face...the way he'd just flop all of a sudden, when he wanted to lie down...and the way he'd prance with his front feet, when he wagged his tail...the way Honey would shelter him in her arms, when strange people came around. The other puppies were sold...one by one...but that one? She couldn't let that one leave home.

When Honey brings him out to the pasture for a nice long walk...he runs around her in great big circles, and dashes in close...to lick her hand. When she brings him into the barn, he prances back and forth in the aisle in front of our stalls...he wags his tail so hard, and looks up at us do innocently. We can't resist the little guy.

As Mister says, "We need another boy...I can't hold my own against all these females." I guess we have a new member of the family, Mother. Honey named him "King Yip of Candyhorse Farm." He even looks like royalty...completely golden sable, with about seven white hairs on the back of his neck...and when kings are babies, who wants royal dignity!

Chapter 18

Groundhog Day Again!

Honestly, the older I get, the faster time flies! I'm officially six years old now...and it seems like just yesterday that I was jumping out of Puddin's paddock to be with you and the gang. Say, what's this I hear about Puddin having a baby brother! And a bay one, at that! How come he's a bay, when Aunt Sugar and Puddin are both chestnuts? Even Gabbar was a chestnut before he turned to gray! My family is just raving about the new little colt...he's my half-brother, you know...because Gabbar is his sire. He's three-fourths Arabian and one-fourth Saddlebred, and his name is "Little Toot."

Where on earth did he get that name! Is he a midget horse? Does he go tooting around like a tugboat? Honey says she remembers a story about a tugboat named Little Toot...a tugboat that tried, and tried, and succeeded in the end. I'm thinking of that legend about bay Arabians...how hardy they're supposed to be, and how fast they can run, and how they're so sure-footed when they go down the side of a precipice. Wouldn't it be wonderful if Little Toot could live up to that legend?

Honey says he's thrilling to look at...with a coal-black mane and tail, and his legs set on like four corners of a box. Now that, I would like to see. She says he already has "the look of eagles"...and he won't be a real yearling until the twenty-seventh of May. She says he's a very dark chestnut on the body, and his legs are black from the knees down. Doesn't it seem strange that when a chestnut horse has a black mane and tail plus black lower-legs, he is automatically a bay instead of a chestnut? A true chestnut can be light, dark, or in-between...but Honey says she thinks most bays come in the darker shades. Maybe they started out to be black, and changed their minds before they were foaled...when they heard that legend about black horses having a rough time on rocky ground, maybe. Ha!

Anyway, Honey came back from visiting Helen, bound and determined to have a bay part-Arabian sometime. Missus said, "No more horses until we get out to the farm!" Does that give you a hint about the news I have to tell? We've bought an honest-to-goodness, real-life farm! Missus says they have to wear their "rose-colored glasses" when they go out to look it over...because right now, it's an honest-to-goodness, real-life mess!

Between Christmas and my official birthday, they heard about a hundred-and-sixty-acre farm that looked like "ranch country." Whew! A hundred and sixty acres! The man said it had been for sale a few months ago, and he could write to the owner (who lived in another state) to ask if it was still available. He told the family where it was located ... they drove out there immediately ... and fell in love with it " from the road. " That's my family ... they know what they like ... pronto!

The dream farm!

They kept hounding the real estate man, to see it he'd had an answer to his letter. He'd say, " You haven't even seen the place yet...how do you know you want to buy it!" He told them not to get their hopes up to high, and not to expect any palace at the top of that hill...said it had been rented a long time and was very run down. Said there wasn't anything on that farm that wasn't badly in need of repair. His words of caution went in one ear and out the other...it was the lay of the land they were in love with... to heck with the repairs!

They drove out there everyday of Christmas vacation... took field glasses, took colored slide-pictures from their car, parked on the road...and when they felt too conspicuous, they'd drive around a few miles and go back for another look. All the buildings sit high on a hill in the middle of the farm. A big square house, a tall silo, a dairy barn, a grove of trees to the north and west...and even with the binoculars, they couldn't see more than that without driving up the lane. Their mouths were absolutely watering for a chance to go up and browse around.

When the realtor came to show them the answer to his letter, you could hear the cheering a mile away! The family piled in his car and they raced out hell-bent-for-election! They were so set on the place by that time, they wouldn't have cared if all the buildings were tumble-down shacks...and I guess they had to laugh when they found out they were tumble -down shacks. They went around looking...saying, "We'll get rid of that one...this one can come down...maybe that one's okay...we'll tear all these fences out...that silo will have to go...we'll get a lot of good wood out of the dairy barn, so it's just as well that it's ready to fall apart...that's a good corn crib, but we won't have corn, so we'll turn it into a horse barn...and that barn they keep chickens in would be better, fixed up for horses...and when it came to looking at the house, anything seemed possible.

Missus' remodeled farm house.

Missus says she'd rather remodel an old house any day than build a brand new one, and when they told their building contractor about the old farm house he was going to work on...he said, "Oh, yes! Most old farm-houses in this part of the country can be beautifully remodeled. Usually the first step is to tear 'em down." But he'll be pleasantly surprised with ours. All he has to do is yank the insides out of it, put a new support-wall in the basement, take out a few walls on the first and second floors, insulate the outside walls plus the attic floor, put in two bathrooms plus a kitchen sink, add a few new windows, re-putty the old, put in new stairways, add on an extra section for the kitchen "sitting room" and "modern pantry"...oh, and a roof for the "veranda" on the south and east sides of the house. Missus drew up the plans, and said that was all she "could think of for this session of remodeling." Mister said, "Ye Gods! You mean there's more to follow?"

The renters will be moving off the farm on the first of March, and then the fun begins! Missus can hardly wait to have it empty, so she can get in there with her yard stick and see if her blue print will fit in okay. She can't quite decide about the screen-glass porch she wants tacked onto the "sitting" part of the kitchen. She pictures a big riding ring near that side of the house, and wants an all-weather enclosure where she can sit and watch to her heart's content. Mister says, "Head for the hills, men! When my wife starts dreaming up her little plans, anything can happen...and usually does!"

Honey says, "Daddy! Just see what your wife did with this ten-acre place...it's lovely." He says, "Yeah! She'll go wild, for sure, with a hundred and sixty!"

Know what else is going to happen? Both Sherry and I are going to be bred! I'm going to marry a beautiful Arabian chestnut... and Sherry's going to marry Gabbar! My baby will be seven-eighths Arabian and one-eighth American Saddlebred... but Sherry's baby is the one I'm really anxious to see. Arabians

Candyhorse Kachina, Mister's darling.

were famous war-horses in the desert, and the Appaloosas were famous war-horses for the Indians. It should be a terrific specimen.. .Arabian body-beautiful, and historical Appaloosa coloring.

Chapter 19

We really have a big hunk to chew this time, Mother!

You don't get a hundred-and-sixty-acre farm completely remodeled in any ten minutes. Allow two months for the job, and you find out it'll probably take two years, instead. Missus says, "Well, it's a good thing we have our rose-colored glasses." Mister says, "Rose-colored glasses, nothing! It's a good thing we have our health!" Honey says, "Health, schmelth! It's a good thing we have a sense of humor!" And I say they'll need all three put together, plus the patience of Job.

The ten-acre place was sold, and we had to be out of there by the first of May. Just two things were finished out here at the new Candyhorse Farm...the inside of the horse barn, and the inside of the house. I'll take that back about the house. It was finished enough that the family could "camp" in it.

The upstairs was all ready except for the carpeting, and they slept on mattresses on the floor for a couple of weeks because they didn't want to go through the bother of putting up beds and taking them down again. That was a breeze, though, compared to what they went through downstairs! The bookcases weren't finished, the stairway was only half done, the pink sink was lost in a freight mix-up and traveled all over the country before it arrived, and Uncle George took up so much space in the living room that furniture was piled on furniture for weeks and weeks. "Uncle George" was what they called the big crate that the main floor carpeting came in.

One thing they could use was the fireplace in the living room. The first time they built a fire, they sat in the dark watching it...and exclaiming over the wonderful, pine aroma of the logs. Missus had to go upstairs for some reason...and when she got up there, yelled, "The house is on fire! It's full of smoke up here!" Mister flashed up those stairs like a rocket, and right back down to call the fire department...but discovered the source of the smoke just in time to save the ladies a trip. He had left the damper off the fireplace shut tighter than wax, so the smoke was billowing out into the dark living room. No wonder she could smell the "pine aroma of the logs!" Ha!

It took time...but finally the inside of the house was really finished, and Uncle George was taken out of his crate and stretched all over the floor...tee hee. They say everything is just the way it was in the blue print

Missus drew...roomy, convenient, and cheery. They still have to tell people to "be careful of that first step" when they go out the kitchen door...because Missus still hasn't decided about the screen-glass porch. Aside from that, they're all fixed up I believe.

We like our barn here much better than the one we left behind. It has four nice box stalls with big sliding doors. Just three of us living in it now, but Sherry and I are due to foal next June...and when the babies are ready to be weaned, we'll have to dig up a fifth stall somewhere. I don't feel any different than before I was in foal...don't think Sherry does either. We were both bred about the middle of July, and it's the middle of October now...about three months along, and we don't show it much yet. It takes approximately eleven months to "stir up a foal." That's what Honey says.

Did you like Sherry when she was up there marrying Gabbar? Does that make her your sister-in-law? Or are ladies in a harem actually any rela-tion to each other. I'm puzzled about that. I hope you became well-acquainted with your harem-sister...maybe that's your relationship. She's a real jewel...always calm and collected, and very friendly to everybody. She doesn't get out traveling on the roads as much as I do, because she's so much older...must be at least sixteen by now. In wonderful condition, though, and believe you me we'll keep her that way. When she goes out to be ridden, I don't kick up a storm the way I used to. What a baby I was...but, of course, now I have Belle to keep me company, and that makes a difference, too.

When Honey rides me out, we can go two or three miles in whatever direction happens to look inviting. We're acquainted with more of the neigh-bors than Mister and Missus are because we go gallivanting so much . I've picked up a new "gait" this summer...it's what they call a "modified pace" or a "slow gait". It's my favorite way to travel, and Honey says it's an exception-ally smooth way to travel. At first she didn't know if she ought to let me do it or not...because I'm a part-Arabian pleasure horse, and not a five-gaited saddle horse. Pleasure horses are just suppose to walk, trot and canter. Five-gaited saddle horses do the walk, trot, canter, slow gait, and rack.

The "rack" is very speedy...and very thrilling, they say. It has a defi-nite four-beat sound. The "slow gait" (modified pace) has more of two-beat sound...with the front and back legs on each side working almost in unison. They actually work in unison, but the hind foot strikes the ground a second or two sooner than the foot in front of it. If they struck the ground at exactly the same time, it would be a true pace...and not at all comfortable for a rider.

When Honey saw that the "slow gait" was so easy for me, and even more fun than walking, she decided, "What the heck!" We can go and go that way, and I don't even work up a sweat. Surprising how much ground we can cover with it...feels like we're floating on a soft summer breeze.

Once this summer a couple of gravel trucks were coming down the road and Honey steered me down into the ditch to get away from all their dust. We were walking along in the deep grass, and all of the sudden my feet got tangled up in some hidden wire. I stood still as a mouse while Honey got off and picked each of my feet clear of it. She kept telling me what a good girl I was...and while I knew something was grabbing at my feet, I knew she'd get me out of. When we got back home she told Mister and Missus about it and they said not many horses would have been that sensible...just part-Arabians, like Candy of Candyhorse Farm. Mister said, "We're not just prejudiced, either...there really is something more intelligent about horses with Arabian blood." Doesn't that make you feel good?

Another time this summer we were out trotting along the road when we came upon a big long black thing slithering along in the gravel...and that time, I was alarmed. Without even a by-your-leave, I stamped on it good and proper with my front feet. Honey said it was a snake...and I know one thing...I don't like 'em! Anybody else can like snakes, but I'm not going to like 'em.

It hardly seems possible that summer is over and winter will soon be here. Mister and Missus are busy "battening down the hatches"...whatever that means. It's something you do when you live on a farm on a hill and it looks like you'll have a snow storm any day. They say it's Indian Summer now, but it can't last forever.

Chapter 20

My little fellow didn't make it, Mother.

He was foaled prematurely and just lived a few days. There wasn't any hope right from the beginning, but they took us to the clinic at the Agricultural College anyway. I rode in the fine new factory-made trailer, and little "Candy Dancer" rode in Honey's arms in the car. He was such a tiny thing, and had no strength at all. We don't miss him like we missed Ibby, because we never really had him.

Foaling was such a new experience for me...I'd only heard about it before. I went into labor about six weeks too soon. The foal came easily, but he hadn't had time to grow enough. I gave oceans of milk, and they has to feed the baby from a human baby bottle with a longish rubber nipple on it. They'd put a sterile pitcher under my udder and get enough milk for each feeding. That way, the little one had it fresh from its mother.

Down at the clinic, the nice young men who were studying to be veterinarians were gentle. They were amazed at my milk supply...and laughed at how easy I was to "milk." After a day or so, all they had to do was put the pitcher in place, and nudge my udder. The milk would immediately spray out in four steady streams. It was far more milk than the foal could take, so for all I know they may have frozen some for future use. I was perfectly healthy...but the foal was too premature. When I came back home, I was alone, but next year at this time I won't be...I was bred again during my thirty-day heat-cycle, and next time it'll be okay.

Sherry had her little doll-baby at exactly the right time...the most striking little gal you ever saw in your life. They named her "Candyhorse Kachina." There are many indian legends about the Kachina...one, for instance, is that the little hand-carved dolls brought good luck and good crops. Another legend has it that the fathers carved the Kachinas in the shape of all the things they feared, to prove to the children that fear didn't really amount to much. There were hundreds of the little creatures, and each was given a personality and a vividly painted costume.

These legends are fun to dream about when you look at our Candyhorse Kachina. She's sculptured with the lines of a perfect miniature Arabian horse, with color so exciting that you have to stand and stare. The night she was foaled, she was nursing within forty-five minutes...and before

Shatka Bearstep, Kachina and the Mister.

my very eyes, I could see her getting even stronger as she drank her milk. Then she snuggled down for a rest. Our veterinarian from the town nearby came to examine mother and daughter...and said to Mister, "You really didn't need me for such a healthy pair, but I'm glad you called, anyway." He examined the "package" Kachina arrived in and no part of it was missing. That's very important, incidentally, because if a part of the sack is missing, it might still be in the mare...and could cause some serious infection. The doctor put a protective coating of some kind of medicine on Kachina's navel cord...and when he left, he congratulated us on "hitting the jackpot."

He knew we'd been hoping for Arabian conformation plus Appaloosa coloring...and he was right...we did hit the jackpot. She was coal black, with a black-spotted blanket over her croup...and the cutest white rings around her eyes. Two famous warhorses, perfectly combined. They went outdoors for the first time when Kachina was four days old, and the little dickens was strong as a baby lamb. She was so smart that she already knew what fences were...she'd learned in the box stall that a wall (or fence) was "the end of the line." She wasn't at all afraid of human beings, because she'd been handled and petted by them right from the start. Belle and I could stand on our side of the fence and watch her getting used to the great outdoors...and since Kachina came to Candyhorse Farm...there hasn't been a dull moment.

Did you see her when she went to visit Gabbar with Sherry? They were up there for Sherry's thirty-day heat-cycle, and Helen had lots of visitors to see Gabbar's fantastic child. A funny thing happened while they were gone...Kachina began to "change her costume." She began to change into a Leopard Appaloosa...we hardly recognized her when they came back home. They say that happens regularly...when a foal has those white rings around the eyes. She's half Arabian, and half-Appaloosa...and her went to the State Fair and won a witta wibbon when her was only seventy-two days old.

She's double registered, and everyone says she's a wonderful "show prospect' for both breeds. It was an Appaloosa "Weanling Class" at the big fair this fall, and our baby was the youngest in the whole bunch, you can imagine how exciting it was for the family. Sherry has to go along of course, and Honey held her at the side of the show ring while Mister "allowed" the judge to look at his Kachina. I hear she put on quite a show...walked when she was supposed to stand still, trotted when she was supposed to walk, and did her best to canter when was supposed to trot. Mister said even the judge had to chuckle.

For such a tiny filly, she certainly has had lots of experience. Riding to Helen's in the trailer, staying there almost a month, and then riding back home...riding even farther to the State fair, staying in the big barn there, going into the show ring with lots of little strangers, and riding all the way back home...heavens, a seasoned traveler and she's only three months old right now. She hops into the trailer as if it were her second home. Mister says that's because her mommie goes right into it...says a nursing foal will tag along with its mommie anywhere she goes. It looks to the mommie for protection.

You know how the nasty old flies hang around horses, and drive them wild? Well this summer, we have some leather fringe affairs called "Shooflies." Even Kachina wears one. Missus measured the distance from the left side of our halters to the right side (just in front of our ears)...then measured from there almost down to our nostrils. She cut a square piece of soft deerskin to match each set of measurements. Then with a straight edge and razor blade, cut fourth-inch fringe from the nose end up to one inch from the forehead section. She added a one-inch strip across the uncut forehead section with a needle and thread, attached a loop to each side for the head strap of our halters to go through...and from then on, we could shoo the flies away with a flip of our fringe. Such a relief!

Sherry's shoo-fly has been a god-send for her. It not only shoos the flies away, it keeps the bright sunshine from irritating her eyes. This is the first summer her eyes haven't been raw-looking. And that Kachina! She's a smart one! Uses her mommie's tail to keep flies away from her whole body. Whenever Sherry stands still, Kachina brushes back and fourth under her tail...it's very evident that she does it to keep the flies away. Sherry has the patience of a Spanish duenna...and her little "responsibility" can do no wrong.

Four box stalls will be enough for us this winter...with three grown-ups and only one to wean. The way Kachina loves her milk powder and rolled oats, it won't be any problem at all to just shift her into the empty stall beside Sherry.

Chapter 21

We're snowed in!

And if that silly Groundhog can climb high enough to see his shadow...he's welcome to it! Not a fit day out for man or beast, and I'm not just whistling Dixie. Mister says it's not so bad being snowed in, because then he can't drive those sixteen miles to the city. I'm glad he has a chance to stay home all day in the middle of the week, but I can't even see out the window the snow is so deep...or high, rather. Not so cold I guess...but we can't go out...they practically had to dig a tunnel to come and feed us our breakfast.

Mister says if we have the proverbial February thaw, we'll be out before you can say Jack Robinson...but the way it looks to me, we'll be snowed in until the Fourth of July. There's supposed to be a proverbial January thaw, too...but there wasn't any sign of it this year...just snow, snow, and more snow ever since Christmas. I'm getting so big with my foal that Honey had to come out and help me get up on my feet yesterday.

We haven't gone out in the big pasture since my eighth official birth-day...the first of January. Instead of going out there, Belle and I take turns with Sherry and Kachina in the paddock just outside the barn. When we had our turn yesterday, there was a lot of new snow and I didn't realize it. I lay down to take a good scratchy roll...and I was stuck. My sides bulge out a mile...not a half a mile...a full mile. I was on my right side, and do you think I could roll over? Not on your tin-type! Being so heavy, I sank into the soft snow right now. Might have smothered if Honey hadn't come running out. She held my head up, and braced herself so I could push against her and get some leverage, I was on my feet in a jiffy, back to the barn in two jiffies, with Honey clucking over me like a mother too.

That's what I like about my people...they talk all the time. Back on the half-acre one day, a woman listened to Missus talking to me as if I were a person...and with a perfectly straight face, said, "Do you ever bring Candy in the house?" Missus, also with a perfectly straight face, said, "Oh, yes. We all have our evening meal together in the dining room." Missus said it was a woman who had five children and not one pet...and to her way of thinking, that was one more family gone wrong. She said the boys in the family might stand a chance, if they grew up and married girls who liked animals...but nine times out of ten, a girl in a family like that would be "no pets allowed." And if she did break down and let her children have a pet, it would probably be abused.

Honey and Sally-dog with relatives.

Missus still remembers how Honey would ask her to keep Sally in the house when she was playing with children who might hurt her. They could be perfectly nice children in every other way...just not nice with animals. Isn't that strange, Mother? Most of Honey's playmates were the kind that treated their pets like human beings, and Missus tells about sitting...listening to them talk to Sally "just like one of the gang." They never had Sally be a horse...she was always given some special "job to do." And Sally usually did hold up her end of the game...that's what Missus got such a kick out of.

Didn't I mention once that Sally was a mind reader? Here's something that proves it. Before the family bought her, there was a huge bouncy German Police Dog across the street that used to put its paws on Honey's shoulders and make her fall down. The dog was just playing, but Honey was 'scared to death of it. Then she got her own little Sally-dog, and the first time that Police Dog came across the street Honey was terrified for Sally as well as for herself. She had her roller skates on, Sally on the other end of a leash. Sally strained at the leash, barking and growling furiously...the big dog ran back home, and Honey was flat on the ground hanging onto the leash for dear life. Ever after that...when Honey was at school, Sally would let the Police Dog come into the yard and they'd actually play together...but the minute Honey came home, she'd sent that dog out of the yard a-running.

She was only a puppy, and not half as big...but she really knew how to give orders to that huge dog!

In the evenings they used to take Honey and Sally out for a drive in the country...Mister and Missus in the front seat, Honey and Sally in the back. Once Honey asked her mother for a handkerchief...and the next thing they knew, she had it draped around Sally's nose, saying, "Blow!" They'd each have an ice-cream cone, and no matter how delicious it was...Sally always got the last third of Honey's. Missus says she always left plenty of ice-cream in Sally's third, too. And Sally would sit there patiently...watching Honey eat down to her share, and getting worried if it looked like Honey might forget. As far as Mister and Missus know, Honey didn't ever forget.

They say Sally has always had lots of dignity. Even when she was a puppy, she never wanted to be picked up...wanted to be near the family but not on anyone's lap. If Sally had chosen a particular chair to curl up in during the evening, the other members of the family would automatically choose other chairs. Sally was pretty good at "getting comfortable"...and it may sound funny , but it didn't occur to Mister or Missus or Honey that she might be just as comfortable on the floor. If Sally wanted to lie on the floor, okay...if she wanted to curl up in a chair, she was welcome to do that, too.

Now Yippy-boy...he's just the opposite. If he can find a lap to crawl up on, that's just his cup of tea! Do you know how big a full-grown Scotch Collie can be? He's definitely that big...and he still thinks people should invite him up to sit on their laps! He sits there sort'a leaning on one hip, cocks his head to one side... and looks up eagerly. If no invitation is forthcoming, he wriggles around and starts over again. If that still doesn't work, he gets up and flops down with a thud, and looks so woebegone that someone is sure to give in and say, "Oh, come on! Get up on my lap!" And very cautiously, because he does know how big he is, he inches his way up...and snuggles down as pleased as punch...seventy-five pounds of cuddly fur.

He's a terrific watchdog, now that we're way out here in the country. He's a bouncy pet for the family...but let a stranger come around and he's all business. My, he can sound ferocious! And I have no doubt that he could be ferocious if the occasion called for it. He doesn't trust strangers, and until he knows it's okay for them to be here...it's "on guard" for Big King Yip.

Chapter 22

Hi Grandma!

You have an adorable little grandson! Absolutely out of this world...and everyone says the same thing, so it isn't just his doting mother who thinks so. He was foaled the twenty-seventh of May...nine days early, but strong as a little cub bear. His registered name is "Candyhorse Ibn Raas Raffles"...and as you might guess, his pet-name is Ibby. It's good to have a little Ibby in the family again. He's a bright chestnut...with nigh-unto-perfect legs, croup, and head. Everything else is nigh-onto-perfect, too and you should hear him try to whinny like a grown-up...a little wavery, but nobody can say he doesn't try.

About a month before actually foaled we had a real scare...thought I was going to have another "preemy"...but the veterinarian said Ibby was just shifting his position. That was at night...and the next day I felt like a million dollars. They even have movies of me taking my daily dozen (exercise) in the paddock.

They checked on me every night after that...and when the twenty-seventh of May rolled around, they got a whopping big surprise. Honey came out to the barn to check right during the time I was foaling. We have a telephone in the barn, and the first thing she did was phone the doctor...then she gave a signal to Mister and Missus in the house. They came on the double... and when the doctor roared up the drive in his stationwagon about fifteen minutes later, Honey met him "calmly" at the door of the barn with, "It's here, doctor...a baby girl." Ha! The doctor looked and said, "Yep, it's here...but it just happens to be a boy." Mister laughed, and said, "We were half right, anyway Honey...it's here, at least."

The doctor examined the sack Ibby had been "living" in for eleven months, and it was all there, goody, goody. Then he came in to see us and said, "You're okay this time, Candy...you had yourself a good one." Ibby was strong, right from the word go...and this time I knew what it was all about, which is a relief in itself. The minute he was foaled, I knew enough to get busy cleaning him up. His nose and mouth were what I worked on first...because without oxygen immediately, a brand-new baby doesn't stand much of a chance. My family knows that, too...and just to be on the safe side, Honey helped me with a clean towel. Believe you me, no foal in the world ever had a whiff of fresh air any sooner than your grandson did!

Foaling really saps a mare's strength...and I was glad Mister had pulled Ibby around near my face. Didn't even have to move a muscle to get started on my job of licking. He had a long, string navel cord...not like any cord you tie around bales of hay...just long, stringy and slithery. mister had doused the whole thing in a bowl full of the same kind of medicine used on Kachina when she was new...did that even before the doctor arrived. It's a concoction that prevents germs from entering the baby's system and causing a "mortal illness." No matter how clean your stall is...or how pure the green grass outdoors seems to be...nasty germs can be lurking around just waiting for a bran-fresh foal, and an untreated navel cord is just like an open invitation. I'm glad my Ibby had the germs locked out good and proper!

Stick O'Candy and Ibn Raas Raffles, new born.

After he was breathing safely and Mister had soaked the cord (got some on himself, too.) Honey helped me get his body dried off with her towel...several towels, in fact. The sooner a foal gets completely dry, the warmer it will be...and that's another reason why I'm glad we weren't lying in the grass alone. My baby didn't have to lie shivering and shaking in the grass while I licked him dry...with night dew falling, to make the job all the harder. He was warm as toast...and the family was on hand to help him get his first drink of milk when he was ready to stand on his feet.

His legs were a little wobbly at first, but at least they held him up. And Mother, I think my young'un was hungry the minute he began to breathe. He nosed all over me trying to find his little milky...and finally Honey couldn't resist. He knew what was in that nipple, don't think he didn't! Hung onto it for dear life, and didn't give up until his tummy was plumb full to bursting. That colostrum in mare's first-milk really works fast. He had the all-important bowel-movement even before he stopped drinking "his first meal"...and the family was tickled pink.

You'd have thought the veterinarian was part of the family, too. He grinned when he saw that long string of black stuff coming out of Ibby's rear end...said, "At'ta girl, Candy...got'im going good now, haven't we!" He's the nicest man! Know what he said? Just before he left, he gave me a squiggley rub on my back and said, "If they were all like you, old girl, I wouldn't have any problems." He meant that I'm easy work with...and mother, he's the very same veterinarian that gave me my shot after I jumped the fences with the board hanging on my tail!

I guess he was new in the profession at that time, and was in partnership with another veterinarian. He went on his own shortly after my board-on-the-tail ordeal, and wasn't within calling distance until we moved out here in the country. When we discovered he lived just eight miles from our new Candyhorse Farm, we practically danced for joy. I'm not afraid of him at all. Neither are Belle, Sherry and Kachina. When he comes to give us our sleeping sickness shots in the summer, he says, "Okay,, girls...line up." He's the kind of a person who talks to you...and keeps you calm and relaxed.

It won't be long now until Sherry has her chee-ild. Honey's taking bets on whether it'll be a boy or a girl...but I'll save my money, thank you...I'll go along with Mister, and say, "Just so it's a perfect combination, like Kachina!" Not asking for much, are we. She went to her first Arabian Show last week, and won the first-place trophy in her yearling Halter Class! Golly, she's a beauty! And the way she loves to have Mister around close...she acts like she'd like to climb into his hip pocket and go off to work with him every day.

When people hear that we have a dandy Arabian-Appaloosa Crossbred at Candyhorse Farm, they all want to look at her. If I do say it, she's a spunky little dickens sometimes. She flares out her nostrils and prance...arches her neck and shoots that tail up in the air...it's a good thing those Nez Perce Indians don't live around here. They'd grab her to match their prize stallions!

Chapter 23

Sherry hit the jackpot again!

She and Gabbar got together and produced the most exciting colt of the century. Even his name sets him apart from all others...Candyhorse Arabian Warrior. He makes you catch your breath...remembering the ancient legends, and believing them. He soars up and down the hills like Gabbar does, with his nostrils fairly drinking the wind. Half Arabian...half Appaloosa...with the historical majesty of both rich bloodlines coming to life before your very eyes.

I'm not discounting the beauty of your grandson, Mother...he's darling, and growing more beautiful by the hour. He's happy. He's healthy. He's everything you could ever wish for, and then some. But it would take the poet of the ages to describe the Warrior of Candyhorse Farm...and he'd have to dig deep into his storehouse of words to picture such perfection. It would take the painter of the ages to put such brilliance on canvas. With the words...or with brush...it would be hard for the best of them to build a tribute to such a sleek and glorious animal.

He's so young...yet his neck is already created, and reaching for the stars. So elegant...yet his shoulders ripple with the movement of powerful muscle under his glistening hide. He's so innocent...and yet one quick glance tells you here is a stallion who could be worth his weight in gold. His Arabian conformation...his Appaloosa color...both seemed insignificant when your eyes are seeing the breath-taking perfection of the horse world.

He's a bay, Mother...a rich, dark, shining bay. With a vivid white blanket splashed with the black spots of his ancestors...matched hair for hair over his croup and loins. His action is high, and he runs with such speed and grace that people feast their eyes in wonder.

When he was foaled, the Warrior was larger than Kachina and my Ibby...large, quite thin, and very fine-boned. It took him awhile to fill out. He and Sherry have had five whole acres to themselves all summer...and young Candyhorse Arabian Warrior has been over the whole thing several times a day. As fine-boned as he is, you see pure unadulterated strength in the boy...and it's amazing how one glance at him spells stallion. We can hardly wait to see him as a full yearling...his sister Kachina is a veritable wonderhorse, and we think he could even top her.

Remember last year when two-month-old Kachina won third in her Appaloosa Halter Class at the State Fair? Well this year she went back and won the first place trophy! Yearlings weren't eligible to be named Grand Champions over all, but Mister was asked to take her back into the ring to be on exhibition anyway.

Candyhorse Arabian Warrior.

You should see that young lady romp in and out of a trailer. She seems to actually like the prospect of taking a ride in it now and then...a regular little gad-about, she is. They say she likes being at Horse Shows, and when barn-visitors notice the first-place blue ribbons hanging in front of her stall, they move closes for a good look. They get a big kick out of the way she puts her soft muzzle against Mister's cheek...she doesn't wiggle...just touches her muzzle to his cheek, and keeps it there as long as he stays near enough.

It's funny how different horses are in their habits. When Kachina is away at a Horse Show they have to watch her with an eagle eye.. so they can get right into her stall and take out any manure she drops. She always plants it close to the wall on the floor of her stall...then proceeds to lie down with her back against the wall. Right smack dab on the manure! On a chestnut horse, at least it wouldn't be so noticeable...but on white-with-black-spots, it shows up a mile away! It's bad enough here at home...at a Horse Show it's a major tragedy. Sherry does the same thing, only she plants her manure in the middle of her stall...because she likes to lie down in the middle instead of against the wall. It really does look like they do it on purpose.

You never could catch Belle lying down in manure...she wouldn't do that to save her soul. But with her "dainty" kind, a white horse could sleep all day on it with nary a stain to show. To Belle, a bathroom is a bathroom...I think I've told you before how she's so particular with her "housekeeping." By the way, she's going to be bred again next spring...and this time I hope everything goes all right with her baby.

Guess what! Sherry's sister, Manitobo, is a member of the gang here at Candyhorse Farm now. The two mares look exactly alike, Mother...the only one who can tell them apart at first glance is Honey. Everyone else has to look two or three times, and even then they make the wrong guess. The minute Kachina was foaled, Mister traced down her Aunt Manitobo...and it took until this summer to talk her owner into selling. If we had been able to look into the future, we would have taken her long ago when that friend of the family sold us Sherry. Both of the sisters have fine conformation...and terrific "color potency,"

They're both bred to Gabbar again, so next June we should have two more little "Jackpots" showing up. Are you wondering what we're going to do for stall space? Well, wonder no more, Mother dear! We have a new barn big enough to hold a year's supply of hay and straw, and six more box stalls. When it comes time to wean Ibby and Warrior this winter, they'll have private rooms beside their mommies like Kachina did last year.

With Ibby and Warrior being about the same age, you would think they'd have fun playing together...but we can't even let them be together. Tried it a few times and decided it wasn't worth the risk, because Warrior was a born stallion and Ibby isn't big enough to talk back to him. When my family saw that Warrior needed to work off one heck of a lot of driving energy, they fixed up that five-acre pasture so he could run it off. Ibby and I spent the summer wandering anywhere and everywhere...even munching on the grass up around the house. Missus remembered our little game we used to play back on the half-acre by the Country Club. She's come to the door and call, "Candy! Say a little word." I'd hear her...lift my head and whinny and she'd say, "That's a good Candy-girl." Then little Ibby would put in his two-cents-worth. He'd dance around and whinny, so Missus would say, "That's a good Ibby-boy, too."

Chapter 24

Horses, horses, horses!

It's a good thing we have that big barn...with all those stalls and all that hay. The population at Candyhorse Farm is growing by leaps and bounds. The latest addition is a purebred Arabian stallion named Ty Gar.

Candyhorse Ty Gar.

My Ibby is small and delectable ...a six-month-old weanling, now. Sherry's Warrior, about the same age, is large and regal. The new stallion, officially three on the first of January, can best be described by telling you the pet-name he earned himself... before he had a registered name. His owner looked him over carefully, and called him "Tiger!" When it came time to get Tiger registered, he just spelled the same name a new way...because The Little Arabian had what human beings call "everything."

People are great for using favorite superlative...short expressions that paint an instant mental picture of the best, the greatest, the most able, the most outstanding...and the small word, tiger, has come to be the synonym that expresses all superlatives put together. When The Little Arabian was a suckling foal, his owner might have called him Tiger just for fun...now, a perfect stranger looks at him and calls him Tiger. It's his description as well as his name.

Since he came to Candyhorse Farm in late October, he's been many things to many people. To the family, he's "Peck's Bad Boy"...in spite of the fact that he's about as good a boy as you could find. Missus began calling him that because he reminds you of a little urchin who had to peek at you through a mop of hair that hangs down and practically covers his face. He loves trucks and tractors...anything that has a really loud motor. He rubs his front teeth on the chain link of his box stall when he know that his feed is coming next. He thunders up to a fence, but would stop in time if it was made from silk thread. He's always eager...delighted with life, and the joy of living. Give him a fresh bucket of water, and he studiously toils until he has it stuffed with straw. Whatever else Ty Gar is to the family, he's a constant source of entertainment.

Mister and Candyhorse Ty Gar.

To people who can see a whole horse all at one time...he's a tiger to be reckoned with in the Arabian horse world. To the people who can't see a whole horse at one time, he's "that terrific set of legs!"..."that gorgeous small Arabian head!"..."That smooth, compact body!"..."those intelligent, wide-apart eyes!"..."That tiny, delicate muzzle!"

Ty Gar is full of contrasts. He gives you the feeling of bigness and power...but he's a small Arabian, showing his close kinship to the famous Raffles...and his power is substance clothed in refinement and grace. To see him in his box stall, you might think he had been pampered and protected from birth...but to see him cover this thirty-acre "playground" with the swiftness of a gazelle...you realize such superb control couldn't have been pampered into existence.

The family has started the big riding ring beside the house...a circle, one-hundred-sixty-feet across...and while the wooden posts are all planted in the ground, the rails haven't been attached because winter hit early and hard. When the thirty-acre "playground" became too bleak and snowbound, Mister hurriedly strung a flimsy cribbing (snow fencing) around the posts...wondering if it would be enough to "hold" Ty Gar. Missus took one look at those thin wooden slats leaning every which-way and burst out laughing. She said, "That's a fence? For a stallion? Ty Gar could knock it down in two shakes of a lamb's tail!"

The funny part of it is...he could knock it down, but he doesn't know it. He has the time of his life in that unfinished riding ring, and never even touches the fence. He has so many interesting things to watch from the ring. Trucks rumbling up to deliver fuel for the oil-furnace in the house, the dogs in their fenced area on one side, tractors scooping snow off the drive, tractors pulling loads of hay and straw, and being so close to the house, he can even look in the windows and watch the family. Missus says sometimes she feels drawn to look out the window...and finds Ty Gar staring her right in the face. He always seems to feel that he's "inside looking out"...but he trots around from one "view" to another like a happy little chappy, so careful of the floppy fence you'd think he was trying to preserve it.

He's just been to one Horse Show in his life...a big fancy Arabian one last summer, when he was two. At that Show he won the "Junior Grand Champion Stallion" title under the eagle eye of a very exacting judge of Arabian horse-flesh. The family had seen him there, and when they heard through the grapevine that he was "available," they hitched the trailer to the car and made a beeline to his doorstep. We weren't definitely in the market for a stallion, what with winter coming on...but like Mister said, "We'd better go and take another look at him...and we'll take the trailer, just in case."

They went...they saw...and couldn't resist. That terrific set of legs! that gorgeous small Arabian head! That smooth, compact body! Those intelligent, wide-apart eyes! That tiny, delicate muzzle! That whole horse, when they stood back and squinted their eyes! They could no more come home without that tiger than fly to the moon...he was absolutely designed for Candyhorse Farm. And it won't be long until his registered name proves it...they're in the process of having it legally changed to Candyhorse Ty Gar.

I guess he hopped into the trailer as if he were taking off on a big adventure. It began to rain and sleet during the trip home and he stayed snug as a bug, and gentle as a lamb. He actually enjoyed all the commotion. There was a stall all bedded down for him in the big barn...just in case. He made himself at home right away...munching his hay like a good fellow...and filling his water bucket with nice clean straw. Peering at them through that mop of hair...and perfectly unconcerned about the fact that he had left his home, and was in a strange barn with two young stallions and two strange mares looking him over.

I guess you couldn't call Kachina a mare yet...not even officially two at that time. But at least she's "the girl next door"...and the plan is for the two of them to marry-up sometime. The Candyhorse Kachina and Candyhorse Ty Gar will have a brood of three-fourths Arabian and one-fourth Appaloosa kids. Wonder if the Appaloosa color will show up!

Chapter 25

Good heavens! Another one!

But you know Helen's Little Toot already... and golly I'll bet she misses this big beautiful bay! He takes your breath away, Mother...and it's easy to see why Honey's mouth has been watering ever since she first laid eyes on him. Many are the times I've heard Honey dreaming out loud...telling Mister or Missus or me or whoever, "If Helen ever decides to sell Little Toot, I'm going to have first chance." Well one year went by...two years went by...three years went by...finally four years were slipping by, Helen's "Tooter-boy" was still not for sale.

Candyhorse Little Toot as a four year old.

Three-fourths Arabian, one-fourth Saddlebred, gelded and still proud as a pea-cock...Honey just couldn't stand the suspense! She phoned Helen long-distance and said, "We'd take good care of him...we'd take wonderful care of your Little Toot." Don't ask me how it happened, Mother...but Helen gave in. And when they went after him, she said, "Just give him time to get acquainted...give him time to have confidence in you...he'll do anything you want him to do...don't rush him...he will want to please you."

And you know she was right? Naturally he missed the only home he had known...Candyhorse Farm was strange to him...the people were strange...and the other horses were strange. And do you know who helped him get used to his new surroundings? My Ibby did. The Tooter is my half-brother, you know. So that makes Ibby his half-nephew...doesn't it? Ibby took to Little Toot the minute he arrived...in fact Ibby was dancing around in the next stall when Toot was first put into his own new "room." Honey said they sniffed each other, nickered to each other, and all in all began to "take each other for granted."

Honey and Little Toot winning ribbons and trophies.

Horses can like their human beings very much, but there's something about the living, breathing companionship of other horses that has a calming, soothing, relaxing effect. Toot has been accustomed to being in a barn with other horses at Helen's, and even through ours were unfamiliar...I'm almost sure he didn't really suffer from homesickness like I did those first few days...umpty-ump years ago. Toot's been here about three weeks now...he and Ibby go out grazing together around the big barn, and Honey brings him down to our paddock once in awhile. We hear him trotting about, but they have to keep the barn door closed because he'd spend all his time in the aisle if they left it open. He knows we're in here and is very curious about the "ladies in waiting."

Sherry and Toby and I are in the original four-stall barn waiting to foal... and the six stalls in the big barn are all occupied. Occupied by Ty Gar, Kachina, Belle, Warrior, Ibby, and Little Toot. Belle is a "Lady in waiting," but she has to wait several months longer than the rest of us...in fact I think her foal is expected shortly after everyone's official birthday next winter. Brrrrr! A winter foal! They'll probably have to rig up some kind of heating arrangement.

Things are really jumping here at Candyhorse Farm this spring. Horse Shows coming up pretty soon, and five horses to get ready. Every time you turn around, there's somebody practicing walk, trot, and "pose pretty, now, so the judge can get a good look at you." We have a four-horse trailer with a fancy red truck to pull it, and the two-horse to pull with the car.

Honey and National Champion Little Toot with Missus.

We have another college student helping, and he'll drive one of the rigs when they take more than four horses.

This summer the family is going to one Horse Show after another... and you can almost feel excitement in the air. I won't be going, darn it...have to stay home with my new baby. A girl this time, I hope. If we aren't careful, the males around here will be out-numbering the females... can't have that! Ha! I don't really care, of course...just so it's healthy. June will really be a big

Little Toot shows he's not just a pretty face.

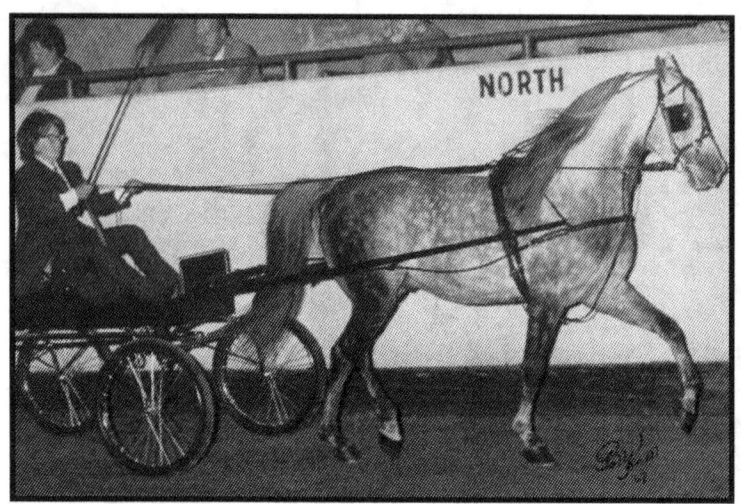

Honey and Ty Gar.

month. Three big Arabian Horse Shows, and three little horses showing...ouch! Sherry hardly shows she's in foal...and Toby's about the same. But as usual, little ole' Candy-girl is as big as the barn. When Sherry had Kachina, and again with Warrior, everybody wondered until the last week or two if she is actually in foal. Right now I'm like a balloon, and they still have their girlish figures. Lucky...huh?

Honey and Candy in costume.

Honey says its going to be a breeze to show Toot in his Halter Classes because Helen already had him beauti-fully trained for it. He follows her soft-spoken commands like a dream horse. Never too fast...never too slow. When she walks, he steps right out in a smart style that makes it really look like he's going somewhere. When he trots, he looks like sweet music sounds. When he stops to pose, there's never a foot out of place. They're trying to duplicate all the new sights and sounds he'll experience for the first time at his first show. Loud music, people applaud-ing, and just in case he wins a ribbon...Mister puts Missus' hand on his arm and escorts her to one side of the ring, very prim and proper. Then he

First Place Winner
NEBRASKA ALL ARABIAN HORSE SHOW
1963

shouts at the top if his lungs, "First Place..Little Toot, of Candyhorse Farm." So Honey and her winning horse go trotting to the "ribbon lady" to receive their award...which is apt to be anything from a rusty water bucket to a silk head scarf.

Mister and Kachina winning again!

The first time they tried it with Ty Gar he thought he should carry the bucket. And he feels highly insulted if he can't go trotting away from the ribbon lady with her head scarf in his mouth. Sometimes when Peck's Bad Boy peers at the ribbon lady through his long foretop, the ribbon lady says, "You forgot your horse, Madam! We don't give prizes to dust mops." Ty Gar just refuses to be serious about this Halter Class business! He knows how to stand and pose like an Arabian fashion plate...but Honey never knows whether he's going to show or show-off. It doesn't matter so much here at home, but when he's lined up with who-knows-how-many other three-year-old stallions with a judge eyeing him...he'd better settle down and tend to his knittin'...that's for sure.

Mister will show his baby doll, Kachina. She's like I was...wants to be petted...judge or no judge. She can't understand why Mister wants her to pose out at the end of a lead rope, when she'd much rather get close enough to put her muzzle on his cheek. It reminds me of Prinka at the Night Dog School when she was supposed to sit, stay while Mister went out of sight. He'd get her all set, and when he'd back away...she'd skooch herself along on the floor, thinking nobody would notice. Kachina does that. He gets her all posed beautifully, backs out to the end of the lead rope in front of her...and she gets there just as soon as he does.

Chapter 26

On with the show!

And they don;t have to worry about new foals arriving while they're gone. Mine came a wee bit early...and Honey said I was just trying to be accommodating. The first big Arabian Show is this next weekend, and little "Nudo Hongo" came prancing into the world exactly one week ago today...or rather one week ago tonight. Foaled slick as a whistle...and he's already hopping around like a little hop-scotch.

Are you laughing about your new grandson's name, Mother? Well I'll have you know that Nudo Hongo means Young Warrior...and it suits him to a tea. He's a chestnut, a little trotting chestnut. When Nudo trots, it looks like the law of gravity has been repealed. He shoots that little tail up like a flag, arches his neck, tucks his chin in...and floats along about a foot off the ground...he's suspended in air at least half of the time!"

The amazing part of it is that he's very careful not to get ahead of his mommie when he trots. I don't happen to feel like trotting all the time...and Nudo does, so he has to trot without going anywhere. It's sort of a slow-motion affair, with each foot hovering above the ground for as long as necessary to keep him from getting ahead of me. I can be walking...and he'll be right beside me, "trotting in the air." If I stand still to reach down and munch on the grass...he can absolutely trot without going anywhere. There's something distinctive about each baby foal...and Nudo's main claim to fame at the moment is his "tread-mill-style" trot. Fascinating.

Honey said I was accommodating when I foaled before the Horse Show got started...so Sherry and Toby have gone me one better. They're not even going to have any foals this year. That's why their girlish figures were so noticeable...they just plain weren't in foal! The stinkers! Here all through the year, they've been fed pregnant-mare feed...living off the fat of the land...and just putting on a little extra "bloom." The veterinarian says sometimes Mother Nature steps in and sees to it that producing mares get a "lay-off' when they need it. The family says, "Good enough! maybe next year we'll really hit the jackpot." Twins for each of them maybe?

Anyway, this gives Honey a chance to give Toby a little training. She's willing as can be...but she's never had to go where a rider wanted to go. Before we bought her she carried children around all the time...children just up there for the ride. Toby could just go wherever she pleased, and the little kiddies could go, too. Honey has to laugh in spite of herself when she's trying to teach Toby to "neck-rein." That's for Western, you know...and the horse is supposed to turn to the right if the left rein touches the back of its neck. Honey can be up there "turning to the right"...and Toby, happy as a lark, keeps on going perfectly straight.

Little Toot in another performance class.

She's pretty good at learning the words and signals...has walk, trot and whoa really down pat, now. But the other day you would have laughed your head off. Honey was riding her back and forth out in the driveway, and Toby was doing well. Then Honey steered her onto the lawn for a little neck-reining practice at a slow walk. To show you how much attention Toby pays to neck-rein-ing...she took one look at that soft green grass...and very, very slowly...began to bend her knees. Honey thought she was caving in at the seams...faint-ing, or something. She took her feet out of the stirrups, and by that time Toby was far enough down so Honey could just stand up and step aside. She was worried...ready to call for help...and what did friend Manitobo do? She rolled. Saddle and all! A horse should never roll with a saddle on their back...and especially when there's a rider sitting in it! Honestly! Honey'll never live that one down. It was so downright comical she can't resist telling about it.

If Sherry had ever done anything like that in her heyday we would have thought the world was coming to an end. Honey could put a four-year-old child on her back...and Sherry would do just exactly what the child told her to so. Honey would explain how too turn her by neck-reining and the child could go all over the pasture. You wouldn't catch Sherry asleep at the switch and forgetting she had a job to do.

Sherry is "retired" now...but I remember back at the ten-acre-toy-farm, when she and Honey had so much fun together. Sherry had a favorite way of traveling...like me and my "slow gait." Her favorite was what you'd call a smooth "parade walk." Just barely faster than a flat-footed walk...and she'd lift her knees, with sort of a springy action. Honey had her use that gait the time they entered the Appaloosa Costume Class.

Sherry was a regular "Old Faithful"...and one day Missus decided she would have a try at riding a horse. She's always been a little leery of getting too close to a horse when nobody was holding it...so Honey was delighted to have her turn "brave" on the spur of the moment. She said, "You don't have to worry, Mother...Sherry never does anything but walk with a beginner on her back." So Missus "swung" up there like an "old pro." So jaunty and devil-may-care.

She grabbed the rein firmly in one hand, the pommel in the other...and said, "Okay, old gal...on your way! Let's show this daughter of mine how the old cowboys did it!" Sherry got right into the spirit of things and started off at her funny parade walk. Missus was enjoying herself thoroughly, and Honey wished Mister could see the miracle happening...when all of a sudden Missus must have given the trot signal by accident, and was scared out of her wits! All her equilibrium gone, she grabbed all the leather she could find...and yelled. "Whoa...stop...walk...whoa! She's running away with me! Help! Run-away horse!" Sherry had slowed down to a really slow walk, and missus was still hanging on for dear life and screaming, "Help! She's running away with me!"

Sherry decided to stop and graze a bit...and Missus slid off her back like a limp dishrag. Honey was laughing so hard she was holding her sides...adding insult to injury. Missus said, "All right, young lady! She was running away with me If it hadn't been for my superb horsemanship, we could have been ten miles away by now...and don't tell your father anything else!" She had just noticed that his car was parked by the fence...and didn't know he'd been sitting there watching the whole performance.

Chapter 27

Ribbons and trophies...ribbons and trophies!

The gang came home from that Horse Show loaded down with them! At the last minute (three days before the show) the family decided to have Ibby gelded instead of taking him along. With his wonderful Arabian conformation, Ibby would have given Little Toot some real competition for that "grand Champion" trophy. Imagine! His very first show...and Toot goes out and wins the title of "grand champion part-Arabian" in a big, state show. Honey's walking on air.

It's customary to have part-Arabian colts gelded...unless their other blood is very important. Ibby will be a riding horse when he grows up, but Candyhorse Arabian Warrior has his future laid out as a sire of refined animals within the Appaloosa color breed. He, himself, is double-registered...Kachina is double-registered, too. Colts not of a color breed aren't eligible to be shown at halter in the big Arabian Horse Shows, unless they're gelded...if they're past one year of age.

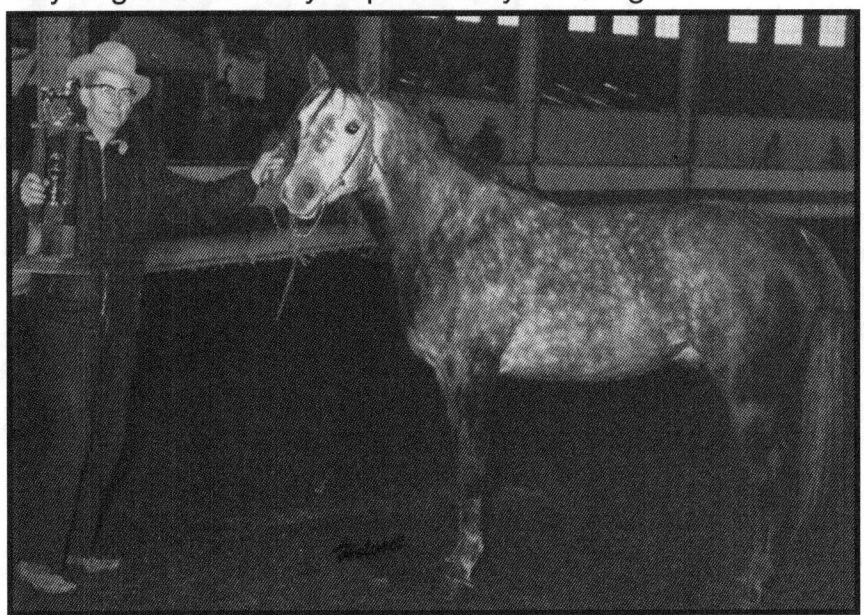

Mister and Ty Gar.

Ibby was still eligible, as far as age goes...but he had matured just right...and for his own good, was at the right age to be gelded. Our doctor advised taking him to the Agricultural College where they have the Large Animal Clinic, with good facilities for surgery. He probably wouldn't have had to be gone for long...but with the show preparations going on, there wasn't time to go after him. He'll get back home after Mister has a chance to rest a little.

Gee, this weekend must have been exciting. Just listen to the results of the judging in our Halter Classes.

First place, three-year-old stallion...Candyhorse Ty Gar!

First place, four-years-and-older part-Arabian...Little Toot!

First place, two-year-old-part-Arabian...Candyhorse Kachina!

Third place, yearling part-Arabian...Candyhorse Arabian Warrior!

Grand Champion part-Arabian...Little Toot!

Isn't that something? This makes Little Toot eligible to be shown in the first National Champion Part-Arabian Halter Classes ever to be held! They'll be held in nineteen-sixty-four...but the time and place hasn't been made public yet. As I said...Honey is walking on air, and so is everyone else. We can hardly wait to learn when and where the Nationals will be!

Who knows...maybe we'll end up with more than one of our gang eligible. Wouldn't that be something to shout from the house-top. Mister says. "No matter where the Nationals are...Candyhorse Farm will be right there flying our colors at full mast. Oooooh! It makes the shivers go up my back!

The family is going to take me out of production for a few years...and if I get nice and trim again, I'm going to the shows. I wouldn't want Toot to know this, but they say I'm actually a more perfect-looking part-Arabian than he is...and Ibby just like me! He;ll be going to the shows when he gets over his operation...maybe he'll get eligible for the National...oh happy, happy thought.

Honey can't get over what a thrill it is to take Little Toot into a show ring. He wasn't afraid...just sparked up enough to look like the most elegant bay horse in the world. He pricked up his ears when he heard the music...arched his neck...and I, for one, haven't ever seen him when his tail wasn't arched. Honey looks awfully short beside him...and it surprises people to see such a large, powerful animal obeying a human so small in comparison. The truth of it is...I think he would obey her if she just pretended to be holding him by a lead rope. He expects to obey.

There were several horses in his class, and the judge can't hurry...he has to examine each entry very carefully. I guess Toot stood there like a perfect gentleman from beginning to end. And when it was his turn to go out and walk and trot for the judge, he stayed in line with Honey all the time. He never tried to go faster than she wants him to...and she never has to urge him to move. Helen would be proud as punch if she could see the two of them working in such a perfect unison.

Missus said Honey's face lit up in a big smile when the winners were announced over the loudspeaker. The hippodrome was huge...and the voice resounded to the lofty heights! "First place winner...Little Toot...owned by Candyhorse Farm, Incorporated!" Her face flushed with happiness, Honey started the big boy at a smart trot. All the way across the tanbark to the place where the ribbon lady and the ringmaster were waiting to award the shining trophy, they trotted together. Toot stopped gracefully...and didn't move a muscle when the photographer flashed the light for his picture. Missus says no photographer can reproduce the glory of those few moments...but the human memory can do it...time after time after time.

Imagination can do it. I can close my eyes and see Helen's happiness when they told her about it. I can see her dabbing with a hanky to blot tears of joy when she learned her Tooter-boy had gone on to be chosen Grand Champion over all the part-Arabians in the show. I can hear her laughing when they told her about Kachina and Toot showing against each other in the Championship Class. Anyone would have to laugh to hear Mister go on...saying, "Next time that daughter of mine wins over my little Kachina with her big bay gelding, they can walk back home!" He looks at the gorgeous "half-horse" trophy especially designed for Grand Champion part-Arabians and says, "Never you mind, Kachina! You'll be bringing home one of the trophies one of these days, so don't you cry." Of course it's all in fun...and this kind of chitter-chatter makes it just like a game.

Honey would be tickled pink if Mister and Kachina would win one of the championship trophies...especially with Toot already having his...ha! Warrior is still a little on the thin side, but he made a good showing...third in his Halter Class...pretty good for a young fellow growing faster than his feed can plump him up! And Ty Gar! Just a perfect angel...that's what he was!

I mean he was a perfect angel when you realize Honey was on guard every minute of the time while they were in the ring. Peck's Bad Boy could have erupted at any moment. He was all brushed up neat as a pin for about the first sixty seconds. One toss of his head and he was peering through that mop of hair again...completely back to normal. Honey kept trying to make it neat again so the judge could see his tiny, sculptured head...and he kept messing it right back up again! Honey was so busy trying to keep him on his good behavior that she hardly heard it when the loudspeaker boomed out. "First place winner...Candyhorse Ty Gar...owned by Candyhorse Farm, Incorporated!"

She turned to the man holding the stallion next door and gasped, "Ty Gar? Ty Gar...first place?" Then came the smile...then came the trot to the ribbon lady. Instead of a rusty water bucket, he won a big silver platter! Instead of a silk handkerchief...a wonderful blue ribbon with bright gold fringe! He was busy trying to grab it when the photographer flashed his picture.

Chapter 28

Where...where...where did the summer go?

Heard Missus singing those words the other day...and it's a good question! Even this beautiful Indian summer is beginning to feel frosty around the edges. Days are getting shorter...and pretty soon a certain little fellow will see a snow-white world for the first time in his young life. He's a tiny one...but him has to be a big boy now. Nudo had to be weaned when he was just four months old, because him's mommie had colic.

We had been out in the riding ring for the afternoon. It's handsome now, with all the white rails. Nudo had a wonderful time trotting around like always. We were in the ring almost every day..."to add to the scenery," as Missus used to say. When we went back to our box stall in the big barn, I began to munch on the bright, clean straw. the more I ate, the more I wanted to eat...and when our evening meal was served I was so stuffed I wasn't even hungry for grain. That's going some, believe me...when you're too full to eat a bit of good grain!

Well take it from me, Mother...a horse shouldn't ever get too full of anything. In a short time I had a stomachache to end all stomachaches. It was my good luck that some friends stopped to visit the family that evening, and were escorted around to see all the horses. When they came to our stall, they found me on the floor...writhing in agony. Honey and Mister dragged me up on my feet...and forced me to walk outdoors. Missus ran to call the veterinary, and Honey kept saying, "Will she be all right, Daddy? Will Candy be all right?" Mister said, "We have to keep her walking, Honey. We can't let her lie down."

I was black with sweat...I was bulged out like a balloon...even bulged out underneath my tail. When the veterinary came, he said he'd never seen anything like it before...but his instinct told him to treat it like the colic...and he saved my life. He did it this time with a needle instead of a tube. And about twenty minutes later, a second shot with the needle. Mister forced me to walk...and walk...and walk. When the others offered to help, he'd just keep on pulling me along, saying, "Come on, Candy-girl...don't lie down on me!" When my legs buckled under me, he refused to let me give up.

The medicine began to have its effect. pretty soon the doctor cleared his throat, and his voice sounded husky as he gave me a squiggley rub on my back...saying, "Got it on the run now...haven't we, old girl!" When he left, he said, "Keep her walking. That'll be the best medicine from now on."

Candy and Honey in a performance class.

Mother, I never walked so far without going anywhere in all my life. By the time the morning sun was coming over the horizon I was able to walk under my own power...and feeling almost like myself again.

I didn't get completely well overnight. The next day all four of my legs were swelled up and aching. They fixed a "mud stall" for me to stand in...and Honey stayed right there running cold water on my legs and keeping the mud sopping wet. It was funny watching Nudo sloshing in that mud. We weaned him right then and there. When he's think of nursing, Honey would take his mind off it...and coax him to "eat your little foodies" from a big shiny pan.

She sat on a chair beside the open door of my "mud bath"...and Nudo romped free in the aisle. He loved the feel of the mud, too. And he got so used to brushing past Honey to get into and out of it that he became quite a "people's boy." When my feet and legs were back to normal, she took him out "for a walk" two or three times a day...even way down the driveway to the mailbox. Little pot! Him started him's walking and trotting lessons when he was just knee-high-to-a-duck.

When all the Horse Shows were over, the family sent Ty Gar away for his professional training...and put Nudo in his vacated stall. Missus says it's amazing to watch visitors when they look at the sign that says STALLION...and catch the expression on their faces when the discover the baby inside. One man grinned ear to ear and said, "This the young stallion we've been reading about? Knew he was a small one...but didn't expect a midget." They have been reading about Ty Gar, Mother...plus all the others in the "show string" this summer. Every time a new Arabian magazine comes through the mail there's a mad scramble of pages until they find the results of the latest Horse Shows.

It seemed to us here at home that our bunch spent half the time going off somewhere in a trailer, and the other half of the time getting all shined up to go again. Trophies galore, they brought home...five new ones from a single show that I remember hearing about.

Arabian Warrior caught up with himself and really "put on the bloom." Ty Gar, Little Toot and Kachina were always "in the bloom." Last but not least, your grandson is now eligible for the National Championship part-Arabian Halter Classes. How's that for good news? In July, nineteen-sixty-four, Little Toot and Candyhorse Ibn Raas Raffles will be down in Albuquerque, New Mexico...trying their luck at the big Nationals. Wheeeeee! The family will be there, too...ha!

In the meantime, life at Candyhorse Farm goes merrily along. We're getting Belle's winter-maternity-ward fixed up. Sherry and Toby were tested, and they're definitely in foal to Gabbar...for June babies. And by next summer, we'll have to figure out additional box stall. People keep asking, "When will you be ready to sell a horse or two?" Honey says, "If I have my way, we'll keep'em all!"

Ty Gar has been with his trainer long enough for the first news report to get home. If you knew Ty Gar personally, you'd get a kick out of what the trainer wrote in the letter. As nearly as I can remember, it went something like, "I've never seen another one like him! He thinks I should play with him all the time. He's like a naughty little boy who wants all the attention. I hung an inner tube in his stall...so he'd have a toy. I had to tie his water bucket up high, because he wanted to put straw in it all the time. He loves to be brushed, but to look at him you wouldn't know he'd had his hair combed since he arrived. He's catching on very quickly...and he's fun to train. I can't get over the strange feeling that it's a little boy I'm working with...instead of a coming-four stallion."

The family had to laugh over the "news report." That little imp of Satan! That's what Mister said. And Missus said, "That trainer may not know it yet, but Peck's Bad Boy is showing up again." Honey said, "Look at it through your rose-colored glasses...Ty Gar's a tiger...everybody knows that."

I could go on forever, Mother. Better stop now, though. maybe more tonight...or in the morning.

Chapter 29

Well history repeats itself, Mother...

But this time it happened to Ibby. A man, lady and their daughter came to visit...fell in love with him...and the only difference was the way he hopped into the box-on-wheels like a regular little gadabout.

I'm getting ahead of myself, though. They didn't take Ibby to his new home right away. Their daughter was invited to come back to spend a week at the farm getting thoroughly acquainted with him, and by the time she arrived, I was living in a stall of the new maternity barn having the time of my life. Belle was right beside me with her darling filly foal, named "Candyhorse Mamzal"...and wonder of wonders, we had acquired Ty Gar's mother and her filly foal, named "Candyhorse Maria." The mama's name is "Shidraffa." Isn't that a real humdinger? We all liked her right off the bat...and she seems to be very happy here.

Ibby's new mistress said her visit to the farm was even more fun than she had anticipated, because of the tiny babies. When she wasn't working with "Ibn," as she calls him, she was out here with Honey teaching the foals to be fond of people. They brushed the little ones, crooned to them, and in the evenings the whole family would be out here playing around.

Had quite a scare with Belle. A man told the family she was "going dry"...because her udder was so small. The veterinarian took a look, and said he had to agree...it did look like she wasn't producing much milk. When H oney phoned Helen, and Helen just laughed...said Belle didn't use an udder for storing milk...said she kept it in the "milk glands" under her stomach. The veterinarian looked dubious at that...said he didn't think it was possible. It is possible though. Belle produces all the milk Mamzal can drink, and sometimes those milk glands stand out like ropes they're so full. When Mamzal is thirsty she just gives Belle a good hard nudge, waits a second or two, then the milk starts flowing and she gets her tummy full in about one minute flat.

Ibby's mistress has flaxen-colored hair...even lighter than my mane and tail used to be in the summer time. It was still wintry while she was here but she led him around all over inspite of the snow...and Honey took movies one day while she was ground-driving him. He is going to have a cart to pull when he's ready for it...then he'll be trained English, and because the little flaxen-haired gal wanted some tips on posting, they had her practice on me. There's such a simple way to explain how to post...remember when I thought it had something to do with holding up a fence?

Honey told her to trot me around the ring and keep an eye on the way my shoulders moved forward. Then she told her to rise from the saddle every time my outside shoulder moved forward. It's as simple as that. I guess post means rise...and when a rider posts with the right shoulder, it's the right diagonal...and vice versa when you trot around in the other direction and the rider posts with your left shoulder. She picked up the knack of it right away.

When the week was over, she and her Ibn were very well acquainted... and did he look fancy when he marched into that trailer. All shined up within an inch of his life, all dressed up in a bright new red blanket, and his legs were all wrapped up...with white bandages, like when you're fixed up to travel to a Horse Show.

Speaking of Horse Shows, Mother...it won't be long now. I'm fit as a fiddle again, and Honey is riding me almost every day. She doesn't let me do that delicious "slow-gait" any more...just walk, trot, canter...walk, trot, canter. Wonder why Arabian Horse Shows don't want anyone to slow-gait? It's fun to do...and Honey says it's as comfortable as when I'm walking. Anyway, I'm shined up within an inch of my life, too...and Honey uses a cuddly sheep skin pad under the saddle, so my back won't look "used." She says maybe, just maybe, a judge will choose me as a Grand Champion or Reserve Champion Part-Arabian...and then I'd go along when they'd take Little Toot to the National Halter classes in New Mexico. Ibby's family is planning to take him, and Honey thinks I should be there to keep track of him.

Ty Gar is back home now...still as cute as a bug's ear but so grown-up acting I can hardly believe it. Missus says sometimes she gets a hankering to see a little of the Peck's Bad Boy part. But Mister and Honey say no more of that stuff...from now on he's expected to be a perfect gentleman at all times. Ha! We'll see how long he can manage that. His head is so tiny they had to buy a special bridle...and then take up all the leathers to the very last notch.

It won't be long until Sherry and Toby have their foals. Wonder if they'll be as fancy as Kachina and Arabian Warrior. You know it's a strange thing...Kachina has always been what they call a "leopard" in color, and now the Warrior is gradually turning to leopard. What a powerhouse he is.

Won't actually be two years old until June but he looks more like a mature stallion every day. These "kids" have a way of growing up before you realize it. Times seems to go faster as we get older, too. It seems just like yesterday that I was a youngster leaving my first home. I could write a book about it all. There's something about this little maternity barn that keeps reminding me of things that happened in the past. I could stand here and daydream forever.

I mean I could if there weren't so many interesting interruptions. This barn is fairly close to the house, and I have to whinny every time a member of the family comes out the door...then a voice calls, "That's a good girl, Candy, say a little word." Or I get a funny feeling that I'm being watched, and sure enough...little Mamzal would be peeking at me from her mama's stall next door. Or it's time to eat. Or Honey comes bustling into the barn with that time-for-practice look in her eye. Or visitors are here for a look at the babies. Heavens! Who'd have time to write a book.

Anyway, the book wouldn't have any ending. It would have to be left right smack dab up in the air, because we keep beginning things around here...not ending them. If I did write a book though, I think I'd start with Helen. Then I'd rack my brain to remember all of the things that have happened since I went riding off down the road with that "strange man and lady and their daughter." As I look back, there are just a few things I'd want to change. Like the time when...goodness gracious, Mother! It's time to call a halt! I keep forgetting that I might be taking too much of your time...and I notice that every one else here is sound asleep.

Tomorrow's another day...and a busy one, at that.

The Horses

1.   Stick O'Candy - A7153 she was sired by Gabbar - AHCR5972 by Fay-El-Dine - 1170 out of Bride Rose - 1462. Her dam was Sweetie Pie A-3459 by Azrak AHCR 2373 and out of a daughter of the great American Saddlebred stallion Prince of Minnesota Am.SB 9669 - he by King of Bourbon - 2822 - Candy had the action of her Saddlebred ancestors and the beauty of her sire Gabbar- she was chosen the 1965 Reserve National Champion Part-Arabian mare at the age of 12. She was all the good and great things you hope to find in a horse and she was my beloved friend for 16 years. Candy was one of Gabbar's first foals and as the years would show us - he produced a lot of champions!

2.   Sherezade F-3721. A white leopard foundation Appaloosa mare sired by Dude Dandy, Sr. F-3325 out of Bonnie Belle - F-98. Sherry was sold to us by Les Boomhower (he created the Pony of the America's breed), to be a safe and gentle riding horse, to be as safe in the winter as she was in summer. Sherry was a dear, she was just as honest as he said she would be - she stood over 15.2 hands tall and when you rode her you felt like you were floating in air - she was proud and gentle at the same time and she was a marvelous broodmare, producing three leopard Appaloosa's all sired by Gabbar AHCR5972. (Two horses at El Rancho Teeny Weeny - too small - need for more land - so purchased 10 acres by the railroad track - this was the Mister's second of the "nine houses".)

3.   Mallard's Debutante alias "Double or Nothing", American Saddlebred mare.

4.   Azal AHCR4718 - Arabian mare sired by Azrak - AHCR2373 out of Fa Gazal AHCR1894. Azal was the smallest Arabian mare at Helen's farm - she was bullied and lost her foal so Helen wanted her to have a good home safe from the big bullies. She asked us if we would be interested in her - of course we were!!! Azal's stable name was Jezebel or sometimes just Belle, short for Belle of the Ball according to Candy. She came to us in foal to Gabbar.

5.   Gal Azal "Lady Bug" or "Buggy" - Belle's filly by Galimar complimented our original entry into Arabians. (Gee wheez we got use to the ten acres and we decide it's too small for the number of horses we seem to be acquiring.)

6.   Ibn Gabbar - our beautiful baby boy out of Gal Azal and Gabbar, he was so sweet, we loved him so... (We buy the 160 acre farm and name it Candyhorse Farm in Rockford, Iowa.)

7.	Candyhorse Kachina - double registered half Arabian and leopard Appaloosa filly sired by Gabbar out of Sherezade. She had the distinction of being the very first foal to be born at Candyhorse Farm.

8.	Manitobo F454 white leopard Appaloosa mare sired by Dude Dandy, Sr F3325 - out of Bonnie Belle F98, she being by Ghost F100 out of Nancy. Toby was Sherezade's full sister - when we bought Sherry - Les Boomhower tried to sell us Toby at the same time, "He told us that we would be back for Toby in the future since we didn't buy her then and he would sock it to us!!!!" Well, we went back and yes he did charge a bit more but Toby was a unique mare. She was the foundation mare of the Pony of America's breed - she was the dam of Black Hand, Reg. #1 in the POA's.

9.	Little Toot - re-registered as Candyhorse Little Toot 2A2932A, he's ours!!! Hooray!!! I never thought Helen would sell Little Toot. We fell in love with him when he was just a baby - a precious bay three-quarter Arabian, one-quarter American Saddlebred little colt. He was named "Little Toot" by Helen's grandson and that name really described him to a "T". He would try and try and try to do whatever you asked him. Tooter-tot was by Gabbar AHCR5972 out of Gayity A2724 who was out of Sweety Pie's dam and sired by Gaysar AHCR 2387. So he was really more than Candy's half brother. He was just four years old when he came to us - by the time he was seven years old he was the 1965 National Champion Part-Arabian Gelding. John Dooley - a wonderful saddlebred trainer trained "Toot" english when he was nine years old and from then on he was a wonderful riding horse, companion, a big baby all his life. We had him until he was twenty-seven years old. He went to college with me and was everyone's special love!!!

10.	Candyhorse Ty Gar AHCR16480 sired by Redraff AHCR4750 out of the lovely Indraff daughter Shidraffa AHCR5241. Ty Gar or "Peck's Bad Boy" as the Missus called him because of his long forelock and his way of tossing his head around as if to say "I'm going to dood it!!!" We had decided to hunt for a stallion since we now had several mares - friends told us abut this pretty colt that Wayne Thompson in Minnesota had. Wayne had several other beautiful stallions for sale besides Ty Gar. We were new to the idea of buying a stallion so we took a horse friend with us named Dean Thompson, no relation to Wayne, to see this colt. (Dean was both a Quarter horse trainer and judge.) Ty Gar was just two years old and had been shown recently at the "1962 Big Minnesota All Arabian Show" where he had placed first in the two year old colt class and was named the Jr. Champion Stallion of this large show. The top half of Ty Gar's stall door was boarded shut, and when Wayne went to get him out we asked "Aren't you going to have to pull the boards down to get him out?" Wayne said "No, he's been coming out of this stall since he was a baby, he just ducks his head under the top of the door and comes on out." He was beautiful, the Missus fell in love with his tiny,

tiny head, Dean fell in love with his strong croup, good hind legs, etc. and the Mister and I, we just fell in love with him. It was a good thing we had brought our horse trailer with us because he went home with us that night. Wayne has said in later years that Ty Gar was the one horse he would never sell, he thought he would grow old with him. We had this wonderful Peck's Bad Boy for almost twenty-six years. He also went to college with me.

11.   Candyhorse Arabian Warrior double registered half-Arabian and Appaloosa colt. He was a bay with a blanket when he was foaled but he developed a lovely leopard body by the time he was two years old. He was sired by Gabbar and out of Sherezade. He was Kachina's full brother.

12.   Shidraffa is available for sale and she has a beautiful little filly beside her. Shidraffa AHCR5241 by Indraff AHCR1575 out of Shillah - Ty Gar's dam is ours!

13.   Candyhorse Maria AHCR27186 - Ty Gar's baby sister is ours. She is by the Ferzon son, Galaba out of Shidraffa, a very pretty little girl.

14.   Candyhorse Mamzal AHCR27310 - by Awi and out of Azal (Jezebel).

15.   Candyhorse Arabian Dream A31255 - she is another double registered half-Arabian and Appaloosa filly - by Gabbar out of Manitobo - she is a white leopard very, very sweet and very, very showy.

16.   Candyhorse Arabian Knight A31256 - Sherezade's third foal by Gabbar - a big, beautiful white leopard gelding. Incredibly beautiful, double registered and a joy to handle.

As we began to acquire more horses my Mother began to get "a bee in her bonnet" that because of the size of the horse that she didn't feel like she was in control when they moved or did anything. She was still the first person in to help with a new born foal or a sick and injured horse and didn't have any fear about not being able to handle them. So we entered another new chapter in the life at Candyhorse Farm. She felt she could handle ponies because they were smaller than horses. Thus ponies were now to enter the picture.

17.   Roxanne - a twelve hand grade black Welsh pony mare - very, very gentle.

18.   Velvet - Roxanne's filly - unknown sire - beige color with a haircoat that felt like velvet she would follow a person around like a puppy.

19   Sinbad the Sailor - sired by Gabbar out of Roxanne, half-Arabian bay

pony colt.

20.   Schnell's Lassie Faye of Silver Crest - registered Shetland pony #39552 a delightful little black dolly, she only stood 40 inches tall - the Shetland pony market was collapsing in the early sixties - ponies that had sold for thousands and thousands of dollars were going for peanuts. My Mother wanted a Shetland pony mare so we went to a near-by Horse and Pony sale in Eldora, Iowa. Mother went into the stands to watch the ponies being sold, my father and I walked through the sale barn looking at them - we saw an adorable black pony mare but unfortunately she had just been through the sales ring and had been sold - we went back to the stands to tell my Mother about her and that we hadn't seen anything else that looked good. Mama said - "That's her number." Who's number?" we asked. "My new pony's number, we just bought Lassie Fay for $325.00 just pay the man Bob!!" So Lassie Fay came home with us in foal to a pretty little palomino Shetland pony.

21.   Vanity Squirrel - Lassie's little adorable 20 inch tall palomino baby. She was held in a person's lap to have her little hooves trimmed for the first time. Our farrier couldn't believe he was doing one so tiny, he nearly died laughing.

22.   Candyhorse Little Miss - A31254 sired by Gabbar, of course, out of Schnell's Lassie Fay of Silver Crest. She was a pretty little bay mare - we had the fun of showing her and Little Toot in the large Minnesota Arabian Horse show in the "Get of Sire" class - the judge really cracked up "That's really the big and little of it!" Little Toot way over sixteen hands tall and Little Miss, at 40 inches tall.

23, 24, 25, 26, 27 - Five registered Welsh ponies we leased from Anna Berensmeyer from Illinois. They were only with us for a short time - they didn't fit in - they were as wild as March hares!!

28.   Candyhorse Inca Princess A57397 - T-88875 double registered half-Arabian and Appaloosa filly sired by Gabbar AHCR5972 out of Manitobo F454. She was the last of the Appaloosa Arabs, a beautiful white leopard with dramatic black spots.   Very, very shy of other foals, she liked to stand behind Sherezade with Sherry's tail protecting her.

29.   Candyhorse Ibn Raas Raffles - Stick O'Candy's first son by Raas Raffles. A very showy seven-eights chestnut gelding. He was named Missouri Reserve Jr. Champion Half-Arabian Gelding when he was just a yearling. He was real fun to show, he was a push button to handle.

30.   Candyhorse Nudo Hongo - (Young Warrior) Stick O'Candy's second son. He was sired by an Appaloosa Arabian named Gali-pat. We had hoped that Nudo would be colored like an Appaloosa but that wasn't to be, he was solid chestnut. He was Candy's last foal she went back to being my partner in all adventures.

31.   Candyhorse Caliph AHCR38364 grey stallion by Gani out of Shidraffa, he was Ty Gar's baby brother and he was a little imp. When he was a foal he chewed off all of Shidraffa's lovely, long tail thus earning the name Little Stinker.

32.   Candyhorse Ty Gar's Tucson, he was Mamzal's first foal sired by Candyhorse Ty Gar AHCR16480 out of Candyhorse Mamzal AHCR237310. When he was foaled, something went wrong and Mamzal suffered what is called a common opening. The antibiotic that she was given caused her milk to dry almost completely up. So we had to supplement Tucson with a baby bottle. He was very particular about it, he knew he was going to be fed from the bottle but it was going to be under his terms - he wanted it under his Mama by her nipples, the little "pot" would suck first one nipple, then the bottle nipple, then the other nipple. He would not drink it any other way and much to our amusement the vet students at Iowa State College informed us that was the only way they could get Tucson to nurse.

33.   Sariha AHCR21015 grey mare sired by Serife out of Arachne this was one of the three mares we leased from Wayne Thompson.

34.   "Vixen" filly sired by Ferzon out of Sariha. We foaled her out for Wayne Thompson - she gave me a spiral fracture on my ring finger when she was just three days old. She kicked at a bucket I was carrying into her stall and got me instead.

35.   Elway Ahna AHCR33997 black Arabian mare sired by Bagdad out of FeMageh leased mare from Wayne Thompson.

36.   Ingaa AHCR16391 sired by Gaysar AHCR2387 out of Indaa AHCR6283, Indaa was out of Indraff's dam Indaia AHCR813. We leased Ingaa from Wayne also. He said she had never foaled a filly in her lifetime. I bet him Ty Gar would sire a filly - he had to agree to us getting her first foal plus the foal she had beside her at the time.

37.   Candyhorse Ad-don sired by Gai-Nation AHCR25408 out of Ingaa AHCR16391. He was just an add on so we named him Ad-don. He was a very correct built chestnut colt.

38.   Candyhorse Naomi AHCR55437 sired by Candyhorse Ty Gar AHCR16480 out of Ingaa AHCR16391. Ingaa's first filly.

39.   Ty Gara AHCR63089 sired by Candyhorse Ty Gar AHCR16480 out of Ingaa AHCR16391. Wayne's foal a twin to her full sister.

40.   Candyhorse Ty Gar's Mimi AHCR53181 sired by Candyhorse Ty Gar AHCR16480 out of Candyhorse Maria AHCR27186.

41.   Candyhorse Americal-pirouette AHCR82538 sired by Gabbar AHCR5972 out of Candyhorse Ty Gar's Mimi.

42.   Candyhorse Bit O'Sweet 2A21624 - Candy's real full brother - sired by Gabbar AHCR5972 out of Sweetie Pie A3459. Grey with white markings - he was a big, big boy and he knew it but he was as sweet as he could be. His first show he was Iowa Champion Part-Arabian Gelding.

43.   Candyhorse Emeer sired by Gabbar AHCR5972 out of Shidraffa, a pretty chestnut colt with a flaxen mane and tail.

44.   Candyhorse Amirah sired by Gabbar AHCR5972 out of Shidraffa, she was the first baby that my Mother could really handle. She was murdered by a vet that shouldn't have been allowed to practice medicine.

45.   Candyhorse the Lady Leonie sired by Gabbar AHCR5972 out of Candyhorse Mamzal. She owes her life to the wonderful care given her by the Mason City Trail Riders, Bob Swarner family and her own family. She was normal at birth but two hours later she was found with straw stuffed down her throat unable to breath, having convulsions, and wandering aimlessly, unable to nurse. She went on to become a National Top Ten Trail horse.

46.   Candyhorse Pixie A15030 originally registered as Hajabara, she was sired by Gazon AHCR9875 out of Dutchess, an American saddlebred mare.

47.   Candyhorse Gay Tisa 2A37653, a pretty little three-fourths Arabian filly, chestnut sired by Galibar 14832 a son of Gabbar and out of Pixie.

48.   Candyhorse Boxy 2A30260, sired by Galibar 14832 out of Hajabara (Candyhorse Pixie) A15030. He was a full brother to Gay Tisa.

49.   Candyhorse Peanuts 2A39419, sired by Galibar 14832 out of Hajula A15029, a half-Arabian Quarter horse mix, a pretty little bay.

At this point in time, the late sixties, about 1967 on, my parents felt I needed a college degree in something so we sold the Candyhorse Farm in Rockford and bought a five acre place near the Mason City Country Club almost adjacent to where we had started out from. Then my Father decided we would get out of the horses entirely and I was given my choice of two horses to have for my very own to take to college - to choose only two from all the fabulous loves in that barn nearly tore my heart apart. There was no real deciding for me - my heart said take Little Toot - no one else would understand his little quirks and habits, he was Candy's brother (I had lost her a few years before) and Peck's Bad Boy alias Papa Pony. He was so very easy to live with, plus he and Little Toot were great pals. Little Toot, Candyhorse Ty Gar and I all traveled south to Norman, Oklahoma for me to receive my Masters in Library Science Degree. Then two years after I finished my degree I bought another acreage in Norman, Oklahoma in 1976 to become Ty Gar's and Little Toot's retirement home and named it Palomar Farm (Place of Peace). And then to my joy my parents joined me and we were Candyhorse Farm all over again.

50.   Pride of Palomar sired by Candyhorse Ty Gar AHCR16480 out of Ambrosia AHCR24611.

51.   Joe Butterfly AHCR180058 "Jobey" sired by Candyhorse Ty Gar AHCR16480 and out of Syna Brosia AHCR78876. Jobey turned out to have to be a bottle baby because he was allergic to his dam's milk and her too!! She bit the top half off the baby's left ear. We made one bad mistake with Jobey, we gelded him when he was just seven after he had sired a beautiful colt, because we thought it would make him easier to handle. He's almost twenty-three years old now and he's still ornery but we still love our grey laddy boy. Red Byers trained him and had him for two years, he was probably the last saddle horse Red trained.

52.   American Moonbaby, black registered American Saddlebred mare, bred her once and got a pretty colt.

53.   Palomar Playmate sired by Candyhorse Ty Gar AHCR16480 and out of American Moonbaby. His name said it all - he was a little bay charmer and real fun to handle.

54.   Ty Gar's Lassie Lou AHCR1224500 sired by Candyhorse Ty Gar AHCR16480 out of the sweet mare Montelena AHCR174852. Lassie came 41 days premature and my goodness did she get the special care. A dear friend Emma Maggard, RN, PhD was her nurse giving shots, helping give enemas, bathing the baby. Emma didn't know a thing about horses but she pitched right in. Lassie Lou grew up not very big, a Dresden miniature of a purebred Arabian and she stayed a baby all her life.

55.   Bay Lady Love - she was a registered American Saddlebred mare we rescued from starving to death at a farm in Oklahoma. We bred her twice to Candyhorse Ty Gar AHCR16480 and she produced two grand half-Arabian fillies.

56.   Ty Gar's Tatty Put by Candyhorse Ty Gar out of Bay Lady Love, this filly was double registered as a National Show Horse and a Half-Arabian. We lost her to a tragic accident when she was three years old.

57.   Ty Gar's Kitten by Candyhorse Ty Gar AHCR16480 out of Bay Lady Love, Tatty Put's little full sister - my little do anything filly. She was so beautiful and she was killed by a farrier taking a shoeing stand in her stall. The bastard never even said he was sorry for murdering my baby.

58.   Diamond's Charm ASBA0081470, alias "Bess" a pretty, small (she only stood 15 hands tall) black bay Saddlebred mare, she was American Moonbaby's dam. She was a gift horse, just as sweet as sweet could be. We decided she would be the first mare we bred to Joe Butterfly. Red Byers, Jobey's friend and trainer and his wonderful wife, Bobbie bred them for us and Bess had her nineteenth foal.

59.   Purr Butterfly 1A0252684 half-Arabian only son of Joe Butterfly AHCR0180058 out of Diamond's Charm ASBA0081470. He was Bess's nineteenth foal and has been a little lamb all his life. He was foaled May 15, 1984 and has just had his seventeenth birthday. He's a big, bold beautiful bay, he stands close to 17 hands but he thinks he's little.

Epilogue

In the summer of 1986, we made the decision to move further south. We moved to the panhandle of Florida, Candyhorse Farm is to be found on a 7-acre piece of land located just outside of Grand Ridge, Florida. The original Candyhorse of Candyhorse Farm has left us a marvelous legacy of love for the Arabian horse and some direct descendants - and some new Candyhorses. We still have the original bloodlines that we started with over half a century ago.

1. Sarhita - Stick O'Candy's sire, Gabbar, sired a lovely son called Sin Goldus. He in turn sired Sin-Shyster who in turn sired Siegmund and Segan - the sire and dam of our beloved Sarhita. She's almost the spitting image of Candy - both have lovely flaxen manes - both are chestnut - Sarhita is almost 16 hands tall where our lovely Candy was only 14.3 hands tall. Sarhita is very much like our "Candy Girl".

2. Joe Butterfly - a direct son of Candyhorse Ty Gar - he's our 22 year old "brat" of Candyhorse Farm. We made a bad mistake with him when he was seven years old - we gelded him in the belief it would make our spoiled "bottle baby" easier to handle - it didn't!!! We call him "Jobey" and he is a joy to watch prancing and trotting across his paddocks just outside the dining room window. He likes to let us know when it's time to feed everybody.

3. Purr Butterfly - he's Jobey's son out of our American Saddlebred mare - Bess (who's registered name was Diamond's Bubbling Charm). Purr was her nineteenth foal - she got real tired foaling and we had to help her deliver him. Well anyway, Purr Butterfly was named Purr because Ty Gar's purr and Butterfly because he was the only foal by Joe Butterfly.

4. Blizzara - our lovely girl of totally unrelated horses. We want babies - so since we lost Ty Gar in 1988 we needed a new sire for Candyhorse Farm and lo and behold we found a lovely bay stallion named Tazzraff's Matar.

5. Tazzraff's Matar came home to us the fall of 1997 - he is now almost 24 years old - he is the new king of Candyhorse Farm.

6. Precedence PR AHCR0492590 sired by Standing Ovation PR 0457557 out of *Porsza 0315080 is the newest arrival of our adult mares and she and Sarhita and Blizzara are to be bred to Tazzraff's Matar this fall and with the Lord willing there will be three babies for us to enjoy next year.

7. The Candy Prencessh (Princess) - last but not least, Precedence had a beautiful baby girl March 19th, 2001 sired by the beautiful Polish stallion, Shadimar, who was sired by Euker out of Kalina. She is our first baby in

seventeen years.

So you can see Candyhorse Farm is still there and maybe just some-
day we will get to meet you. Come see us, the coffee pot is on.

El Rancho Teeny Weeny
Highway 106
Mason City, Iowa
This was the first Candyhorse Farm.

The Taft Street Ten Acre Farm
Taft Street (next to railroad tracks)
Mason City, Iowa
The second Candyhorse Farm.

The Dream Farm
Rural Route 1
Rockford, Iowa
The third Candyhorse Farm.

Palomar Farm
1919 Northeast 60th Avenue
Norman, Oklahoma
Retirement home for Ty Gar and
Little Toot
The fourth Candyhorse Farm

International Arabian Horse Association
224 EAST OLIVE AVENUE BURBANK, CALIFORNIA, U.S.A.

DUPLICATE

THE HALF-ARABIAN REGISTRY

2 A 7153

This is to Certify that the Chestnut Mare Classification: 3/4 Arabian
named STICK O' CANDY foaled June 12, 1953 , by the
registered Arabian Horse Gabbar , No. 5972 Arabian Stud Book
Bred by Mrs. C.L. Sinclair is duly registered in THE HALF-ARABIAN REGISTRY.

BREEDING OR TYPE OF DAM

Azrek, AHCR 2373

Sweetie Pie, A 3459
BREEDER OF DAM

Pat
BREEDER

BREEDER

REGISTRAR

Issued to Candyhorse Farm, Inc.
Rockford, Iowa

Nov. 21, 1962

RED SEAL DENOTES: ½ ARABIAN BLUE SEAL DENOTES ¾ ARABIAN GOLD SEAL DENOTES: ⅞ ARABIAN OR MORE
The number preceding the A in the registration number indicates the number of purebred crosses.

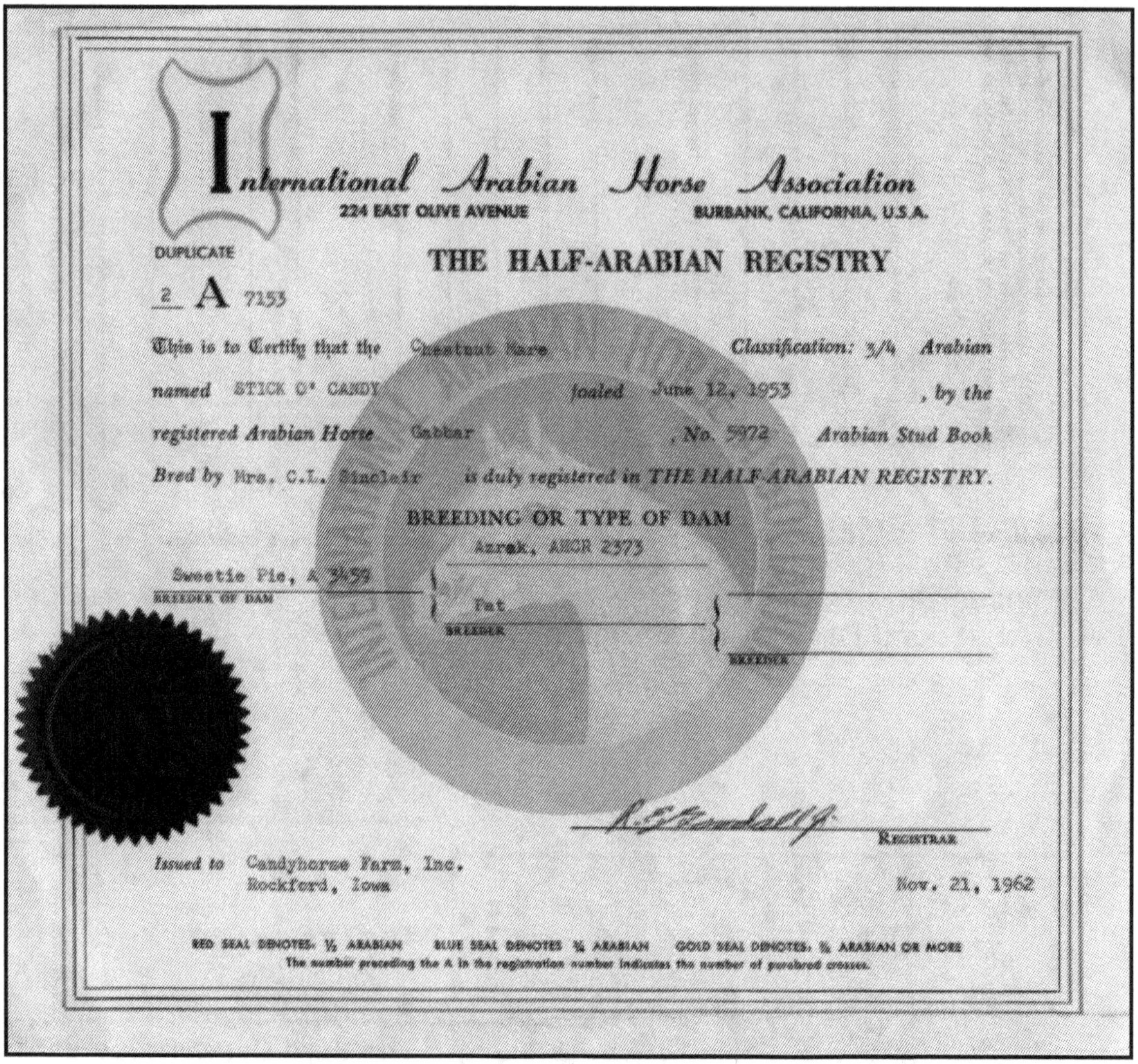

Stick O'Candy's Registration Papers.

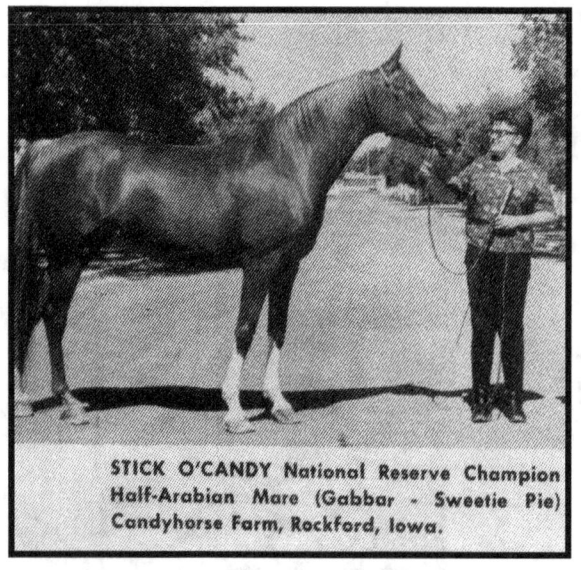

STICK O'CANDY National Reserve Champion Half-Arabian Mare (Gabbar - Sweetie Pie) Candyhorse Farm, Rockford, Iowa.

Stick O'Candy's picture from the first National Championship Half-Arabian Horse Show held in New Mexico in 1965. This picture was published in the Arabian Horse Journal in August, 1965. She is pictured with her friend and companion , Honey (aka Jane Hamilton).

Honey at 15 at the El Rancho Teeny Weeny

Candy in English Pleasure at the Iowa Arabian Horse Show 1965

Honey and Prinka enjoying each other's company.

Candy with Lynn Berry aboard.

Stick O'Candy with Honey and Missus in the yard.

Stick O'Candy

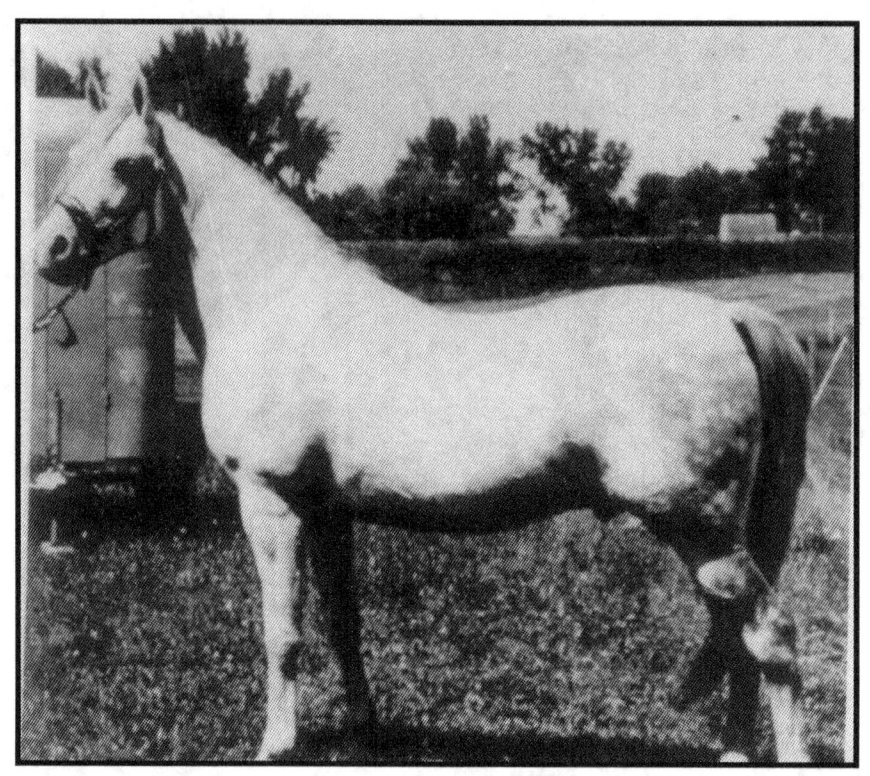

Gabbar (Fay-el-dine x Bride Rose)

Gabbar (Fay-el-dine x Bride Rose)

Show program from Stick
O'Candy's first horse show.

Eight Candyhorses were exhibit-
ed at this show.

Class 13
HALF OR ANGLO ARABIAN FILLIES AND MARES (Any age)

Four Ribbons

No.	Horse	Owner
4	STICK O'CANDY	Robert W. Hamilton, Mason City, Iowa
5	GAYLA ROSE	Terry Pieper, Rose Creek, Minn.
9	SU-KARRAH	Carol & Susan Landmesser, Stillwater, Minn
13	RENAY	Robert Erdman, West Concord, Minn.
20	PHANTOM MISS	Ann Garvais, Excelsior, Minn.
35	PENRAM	Robert Luger, St. Croix Falls, Wisc.
40	TIMBER HILLS GOLDEN STARLETT	Mrs. L. G. Peterson, Hopkins, Minn.

Stick O'Candy's first class in the Minnesota All Arabian Horse Show.

CANDYHORSE LITTLE TOOT, Champion Half-
Arab Gelding. See "On The Cover" page 4.

This photo of Candyhorse
Little Toot, Honey and the
Missus after he had captured
the National Championship
for Half-Arabian Geldings in
the first Part-Arabian National
Championship Horse Show
held in New Mexico in 1965.

This photo is of
Candyhorse Little Toot
(Gabbar x Gayity) when he
was purchased from
Sinclair Arabians in
Hayward, Minnesota

Candyhorse Little Toot
with John Dooley taking in
the sights at the Pillsbury
Farm Estate in Mound,
Minnesota.

Candyhorse Little Toot and
Honey at the Pillsbury Farm
Estate show off his "look of
eagles".

Stick O' Candy's 1965 invitation to the National Half-Arabian
Championships held in Albuquerque, New Mexico.

Little Toot's Invitation to take the Half-Arabian Gelding Championship.

THE INTERNATIONAL

50c

Arabian Horse

VOLUME 8   AUGUST 1965   NUMBER 1

NATIONAL CHAMPION HALF ARABIANS

Candyhorse Little Toot featured on the cover of the August, 1965 issue of the International Arabian Horse magazine in recognition of his recent National Half-Arabian Championship in New Mexico.

"STICK O' CANDY"

Shown two or three times as a youngster, winning blue ribbons. Used as a pleasure horse (and had three foals), until 1965 when she was shown at Iowa All Arabian Show.

1965 - Grand Champion part-Arabian Mare, Iowa All Arabian Show

"Reserve National Champion Mare, National part-Arabian Championship Halter Classes, Albuquerque, New Mexico

Mrs. Robert W. Hamilton, Candyhorse Farms, Inc., Rockford, Iowa comments:

"We love this mare!

We don't risk letting a day go by without serving her three nutritional meals which include Pace."

Kraft Foods used Stick O'Candy and The Candyhorse Farm in their advertising campaigns in the late 1960's.

The pony experiment, this was the Missus's Welsh pony herd.

Honey with Schnell's Lassie Fay of Silver Crest and Candyhorse Little Miss (Gabbar x Schnell's Lassie Fay of Silver Crest)

Candyhorse Mamzal (Awi x Azal) and Candyhorse Maria (Galaba x Shidraffa) in the riding paddock.

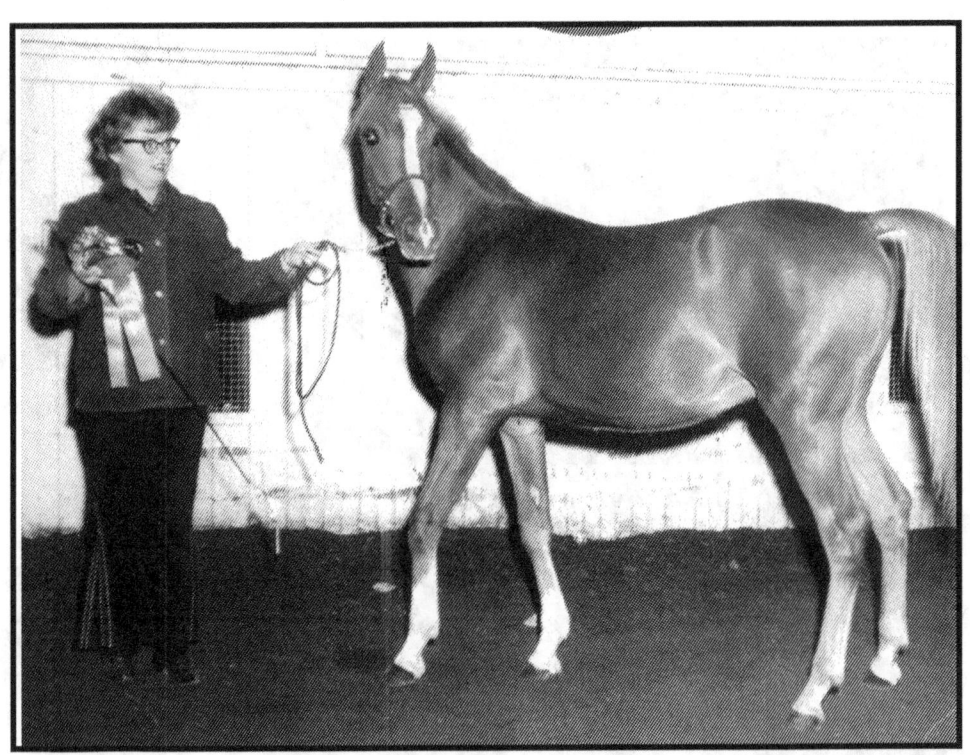

Candyhorse Ibn Raas Raffles (Raas Raffles x Stick O'Candy) and Honey winning at halter.

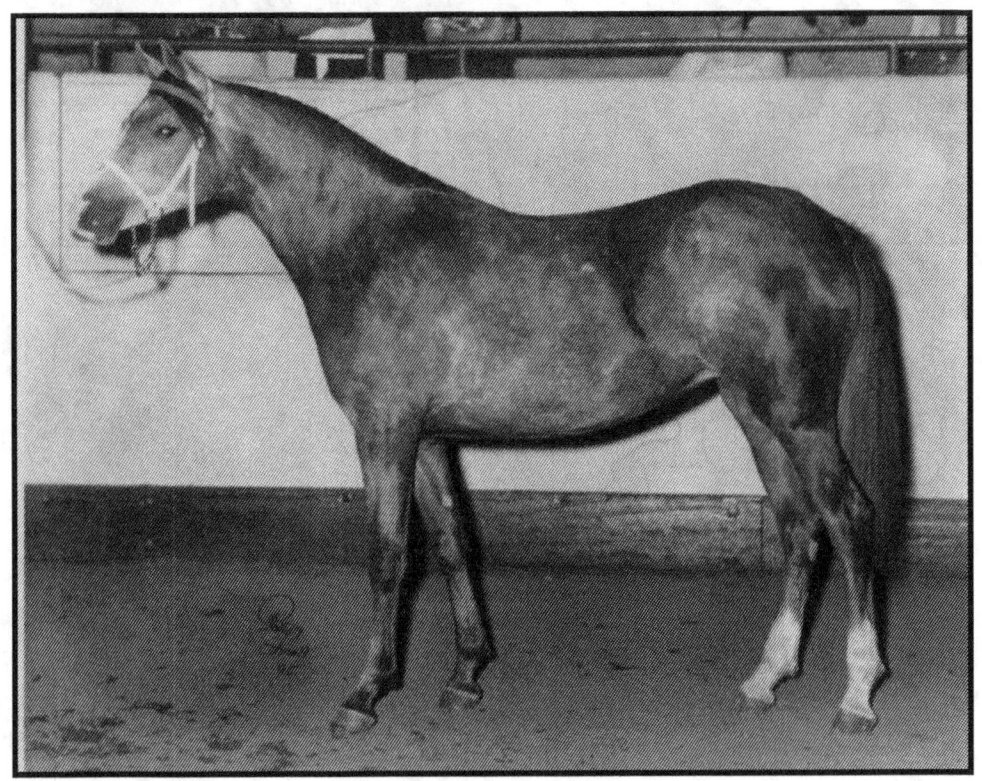

Candyhorse Maria (Galaba x Shidraffa)

Prinka, Scotch Collie

Sherezade and Candyhorse Arabian Knight's birth.

Sherezade and Candyhorse Arabian Knight

Honey & Sir Robert, an American Saddlebred this is the family's first horse

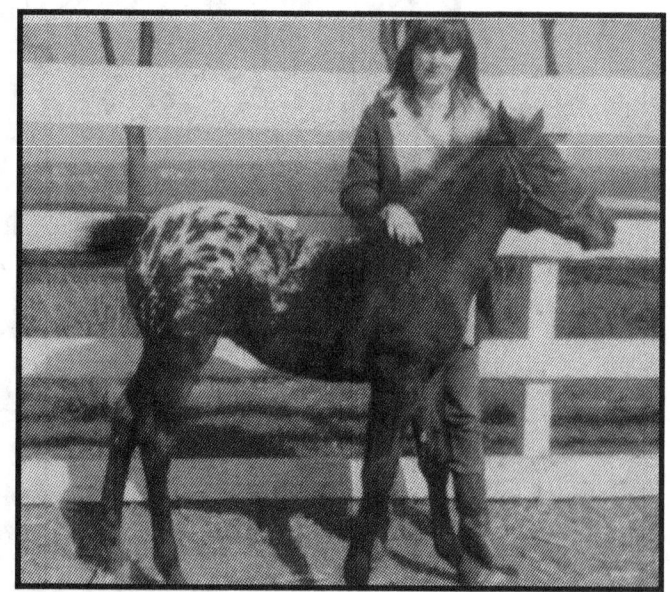

Candyhorse Inca Princess (Gabbar x Manitobo) with Suzette.

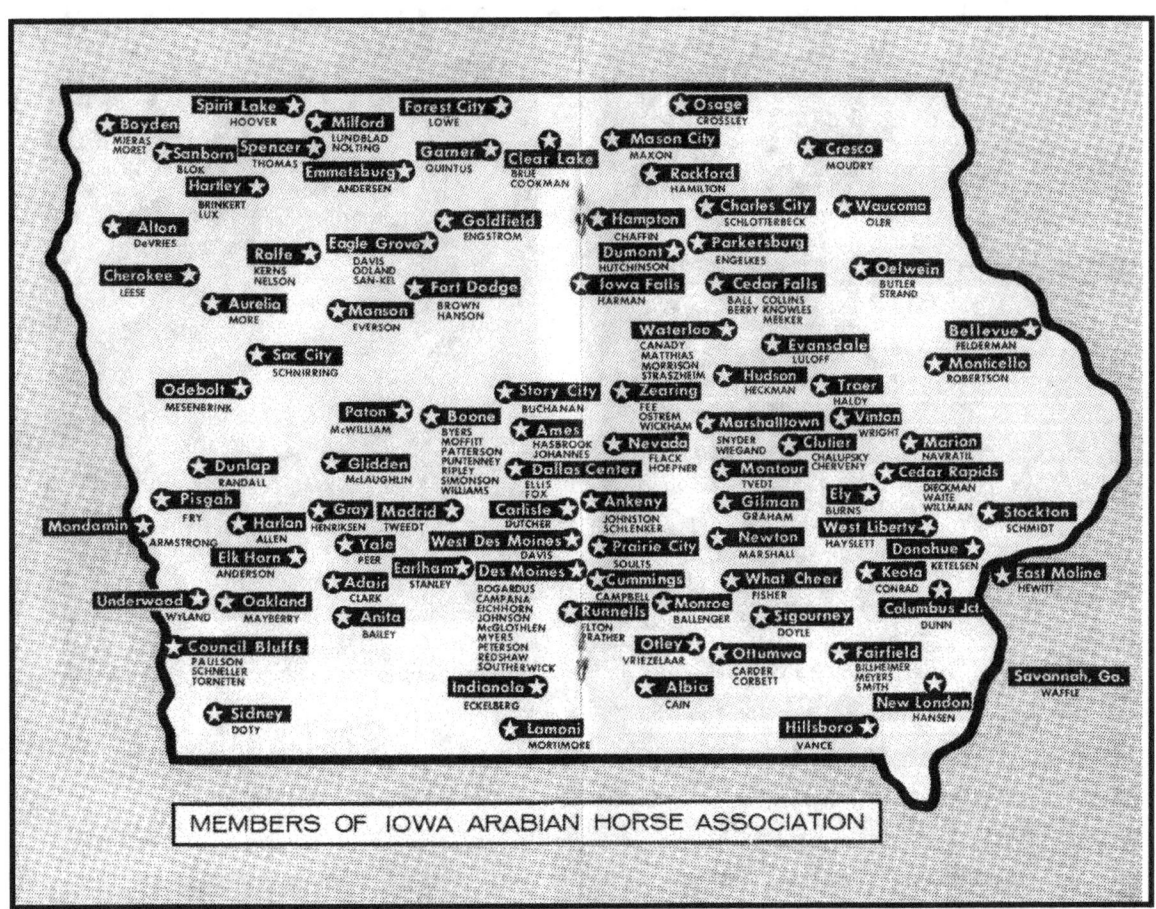

Membership map from the Iowa Arabian Horse Association, 1964.

Kraft Foods publicity picture of Bob and Dorothy Hamilton with Candyhorse Arabian Dream (Gabbar x Manitobo)

Mister and Candyhorse Maria showing off.

Mister and Sariha, leased from Wayne Thompson.

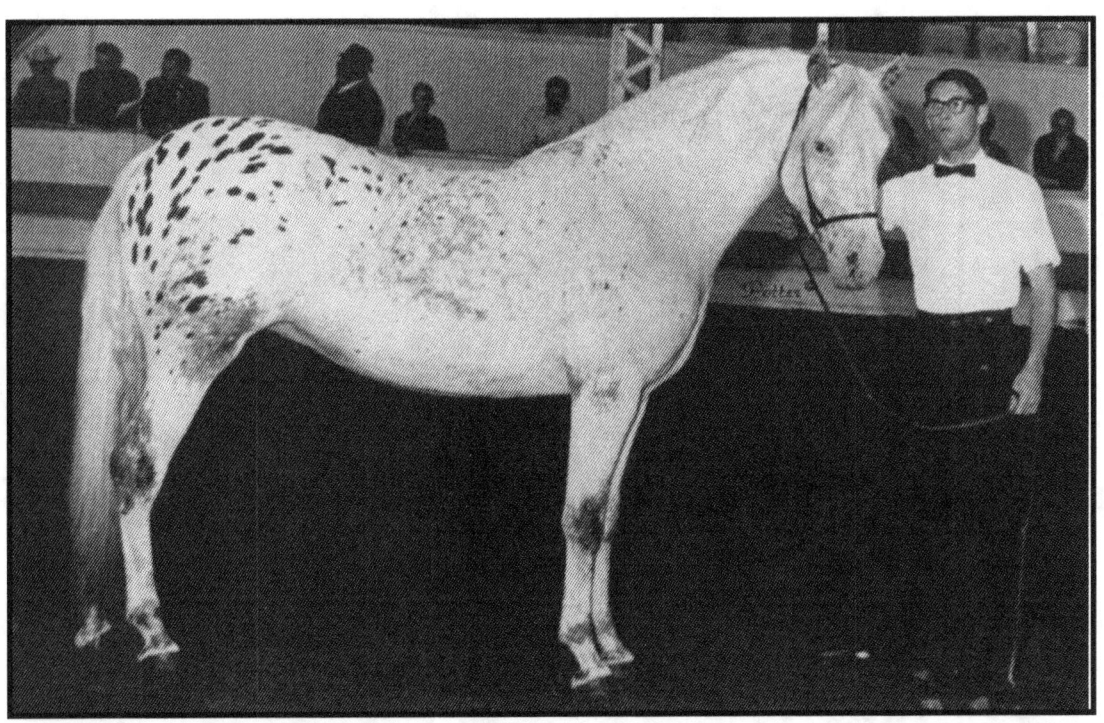

Candyhorse Arabian Dream (Gabbar x Manitobo) with a student from Hamilton College at the Iowa Arabian Horse Show in 1964.

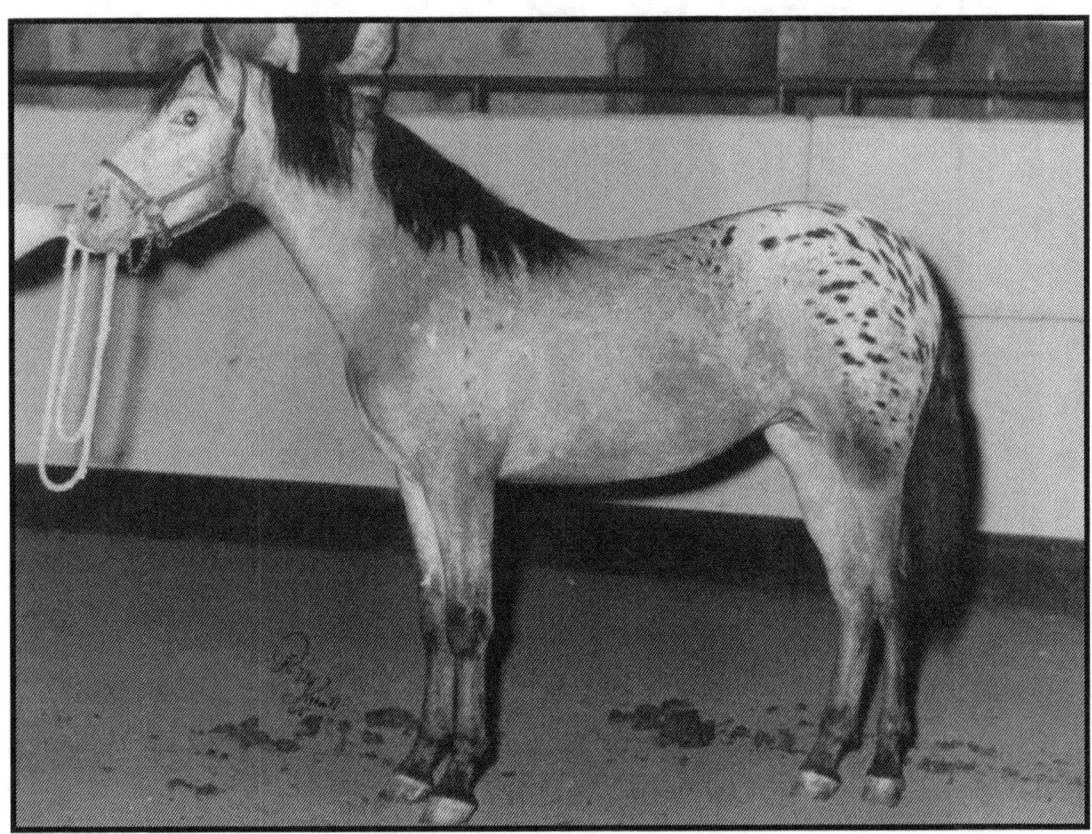

Candyhorse Arabian Dream (Gabbar x Manitobo)

HALDY, DR. & MRS. W. F. & FAMILY, SILVER SHADOWS ARABIANS   106 Mill St., Traer 50675   Ph: 8-2559

Waraq	31952	bay M	Warande x Shabraq
Ghaytar	A42220	ch. G	½ by Ibn Gayid

HAMILTON, MR,. & MRS,. ROBERT W. & JANE, CANDYHORSE FARM INC.   Rt. 2, Rockford 50468   Ph: 515-756-3537

Candyhorse Ty Gar	16480	gr. S	Redraff x Shidraffa
Candyhorse Maria	27186	ch. M	Galaba x Shidraffa
Candyhorse Mamzal	27310	gr. M	Awi x Azal
Azal	4718	gr. M	Azrak x Fa Gazal
Shidraffa	5241	gr. M	Indraff x Shillah
Candyhorse Caliph	38364	gr. S	Gani x Shidraffa
Candyhorse Arabian Knight	A31256	ap. S	½ by Gabbar
Candyhorse Arabian Dream	A31255	ap. M	½ by Gabbar
Candyhorse Little Miss	A31254	bay M	½ by Gabbar
Candyhorse Little Toot	2A29328	bay G	¾ by Gabbar
Stick O' Candy	A7153	ch. M	¾ by Gabbar

(On lease from Wayne Thompson)

Sariha	21015	gr. M	Serife x Arachne
Filly	pending	gr. M	Ferzon x Sariha
Elway Ahna	33997	blk. M	Bagdad x Fe Mageh

HANSON, LLOYD, LOUISE, DALE, KATHLEEN   Rt. 3, Ft. Dodge 50501   Ph: 576-2978

Elmwood's Folly	19007	bay M	Na-Aiyil x Joy
Riftezza	2A20851	ch. M	¾ by Riftez

HASBROOK, RICHARD & CAROLYN   3717 Ross Rd., Ames   Ph: 292-3075

Azja	17885	bay M	Razja x Capriola
Narzja	29099	ch. M	El Nar x Azja
Aztra	32631	bay M	Rasoulmatall x Azja
☐ Azjure	36502	bay S	Azraff x Azja

HAYSLETT, MR. & MRS. E. C.   Rt. 2, Box 224, West Liberty 52776   Ph: 627-2606

@Basha Barif	28049	gr. S	Hassan Ibn Rasoulmatall x Lotna
☐Billel	36303	gr. S	Rasoulmatall x Esperanzo Turissa
Rafhariss	35140	gr. G	Rafhar x Esperanzo Turissa
Esperanzo Turissa	17118	gr. M	Faaris x Star of Raftur

HENRIKSEN ARABIANS, RUTH & DALE HENRIKSEN   Rt. 1, Gray 50110   Ph: 712-563-3907

Komijne	8777	ch. M	Handeyraff x Carousel
Comar Mirfijne	19083	gr. M	Mirfey x Komijne
Comar Azmijne	26605	gr. M	Azraff x Komijne
Raffmijne	28287	gr. M	Azraff x Komijne
Hello Dahling	32609	bay M	Azraff x Komijne
☐ Dijne	38003	bay M	Azraff x Komijne
☐ Azmiraff	38002	gr. S	Azraff x Comar Mirfijne

38

Iowa Arabian Horse Membership directory.

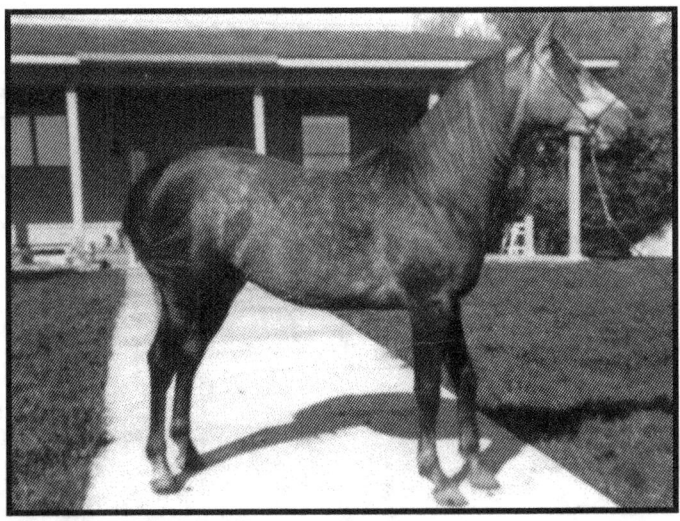

Candyhorse Ty Gar as a two year old, just after he won 1962 Jr. Champion Stallion of the Minnesota Arabian Horse Show.

Candyhorse Ty Gar at age 23 with Honey aboard.

Candyhorse Ty Gar and John Dooley, practicing for the halter class.

Candyhorse Ty Gar at age 20.

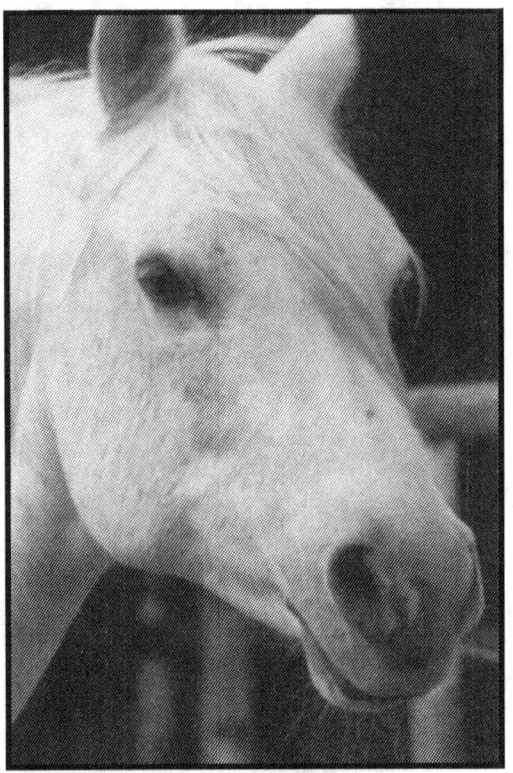

Candyhorse Ty Gar at age 22.

Ty Gar and John Dooley at the Pillsbury Farm Estate

Ty Gar saying "a little word".

Suzette Wyman, my sister.

Honey and Ty Gar (age 24)

Candyhorse Ty Gar and Dean Thompson in costume at KGLO Channel 3 Television Station in Mason City, Iowa for a special, live program highlighting Candyhorse Farm of Rockford, Iowa.

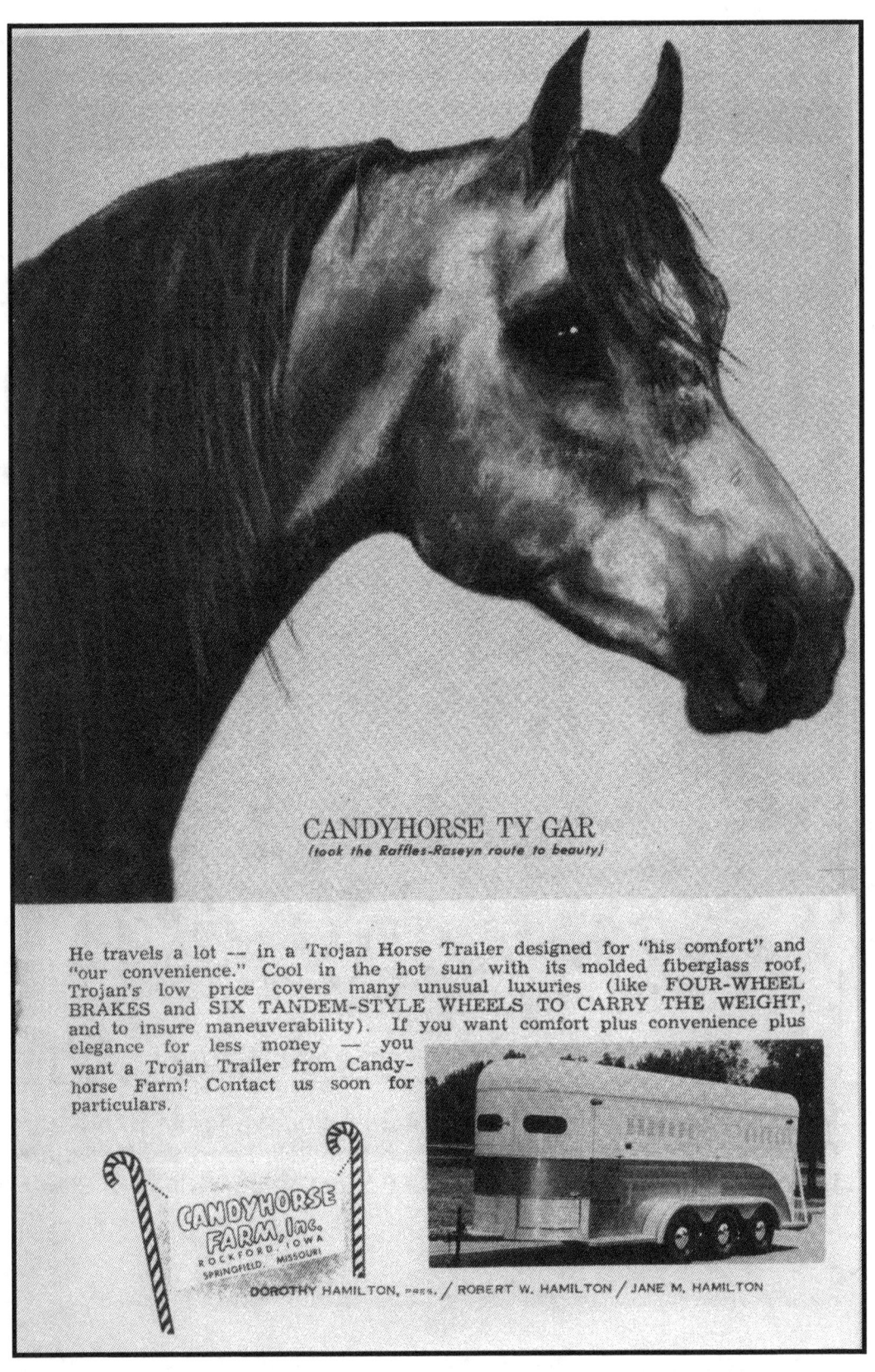

CANDYHORSE TY GAR
(took the Raffles-Raseyn route to beauty)

He travels a lot -- in a Trojan Horse Trailer designed for "his comfort" and "our convenience." Cool in the hot sun with its molded fiberglass roof, Trojan's low price covers many unusual luxuries (like FOUR-WHEEL BRAKES and SIX TANDEM-STYLE WHEELS TO CARRY THE WEIGHT, and to insure maneuverability). If you want comfort plus convenience plus elegance for less money — you want a Trojan Trailer from Candyhorse Farm! Contact us soon for particulars.

CANDYHORSE FARM, Inc.
ROCKFORD, IOWA
SPRINGFIELD, MISSOURI

DOROTHY HAMILTON, PRES. / ROBERT W. HAMILTON / JANE M. HAMILTON

Publicity advertisement for Ty Gar and Trojan trailers, using the head study done by Emilie Touraine of Scottsdale, Arizona.

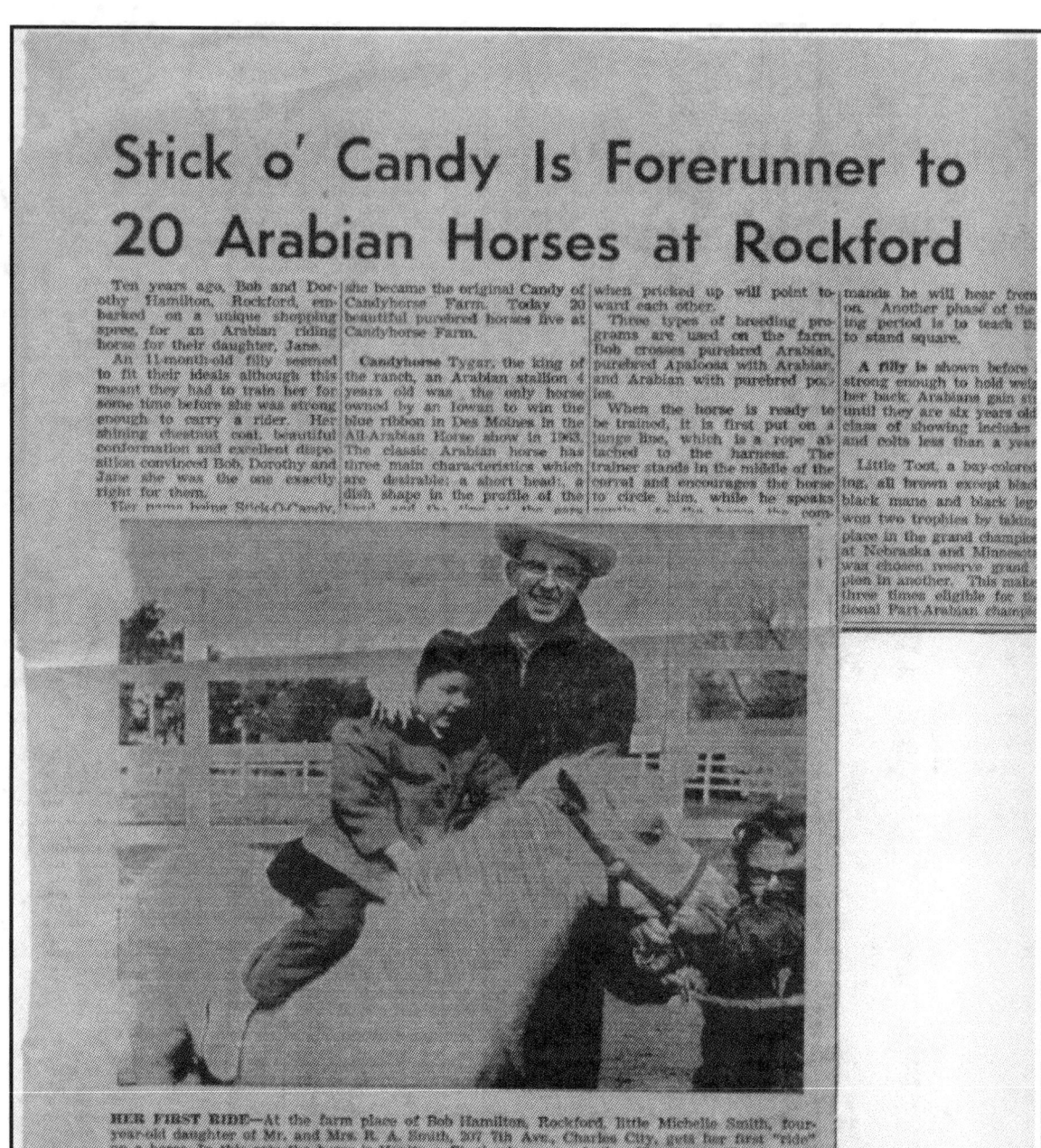

Stick o' Candy Is Forerunner to 20 Arabian Horses at Rockford

Ten years ago, Bob and Dorothy Hamilton, Rockford, embarked on a unique shopping spree, for an Arabian riding horse for their daughter, Jane.

An 11-month-old filly seemed to fit their ideals although this meant they had to train her for some time before she was strong enough to carry a rider. Her shining chestnut coat, beautiful conformation and excellent disposition convinced Bob, Dorothy and Jane she was the one exactly right for them.

Her name being Stick-O'Candy,

she became the original Candy of Candyhorse Farm. Today 20 beautiful purebred horses live at Candyhorse Farm.

Candyhorse Tygar, the king of the ranch, an Arabian stallion 4 years old was the only horse owned by an Iowan to win the blue ribbon in Des Moines in the All-Arabian Horse show in 1963. The classic Arabian horse has three main characteristics which are desirable: a short head, a dish shape in the profile of the

when pricked up will point toward each other.

Three types of breeding programs are used on the farm. Bob crosses purebred Arabian, purebred Apaloosa with Arabian, and Arabian with purebred ponies.

When the horse is ready to be trained, it is first put on a lunge line, which is a rope attached to the harness. The trainer stands in the middle of the corral and encourages the horse to circle him, while he speaks

mands he will hear from on. Another phase of the ing period is to teach th to stand square.

A filly is shown before strong enough to hold weig her back. Arabians gain st until they are six years old class of showing includes and colts less than a year

Little Toot, a bay-colored ing, all brown except blac black mane and black leg won two trophies by takin place in the grand champio at Nebraska and Minnesot was chosen reserve grand pion in another. This make three times eligible for th tional Part-Arabian champi

HER FIRST RIDE—At the farm place of Bob Hamilton, Rockford, little Michelle Smith, four-year-old daughter of Mr. and Mrs. R. A. Smith, 307 7th Ave., Charles City, gets her first "ride" on a horse. In this case the horse is Vanity, a Shetland pony of the Hamiltons. Hamilton is shown assisting Michelle, while Jane Hamilton, is at right holding the bridle.—(Pressphoto)

Many newspaper articles were written highlighting the Candyhorse Farm. Pictured in this article is Mister (Bob Hamilton) and Vanity Squirrel, a registered Shetland pony, daughter of Schnell's Lassie Fay of Silver Crest.

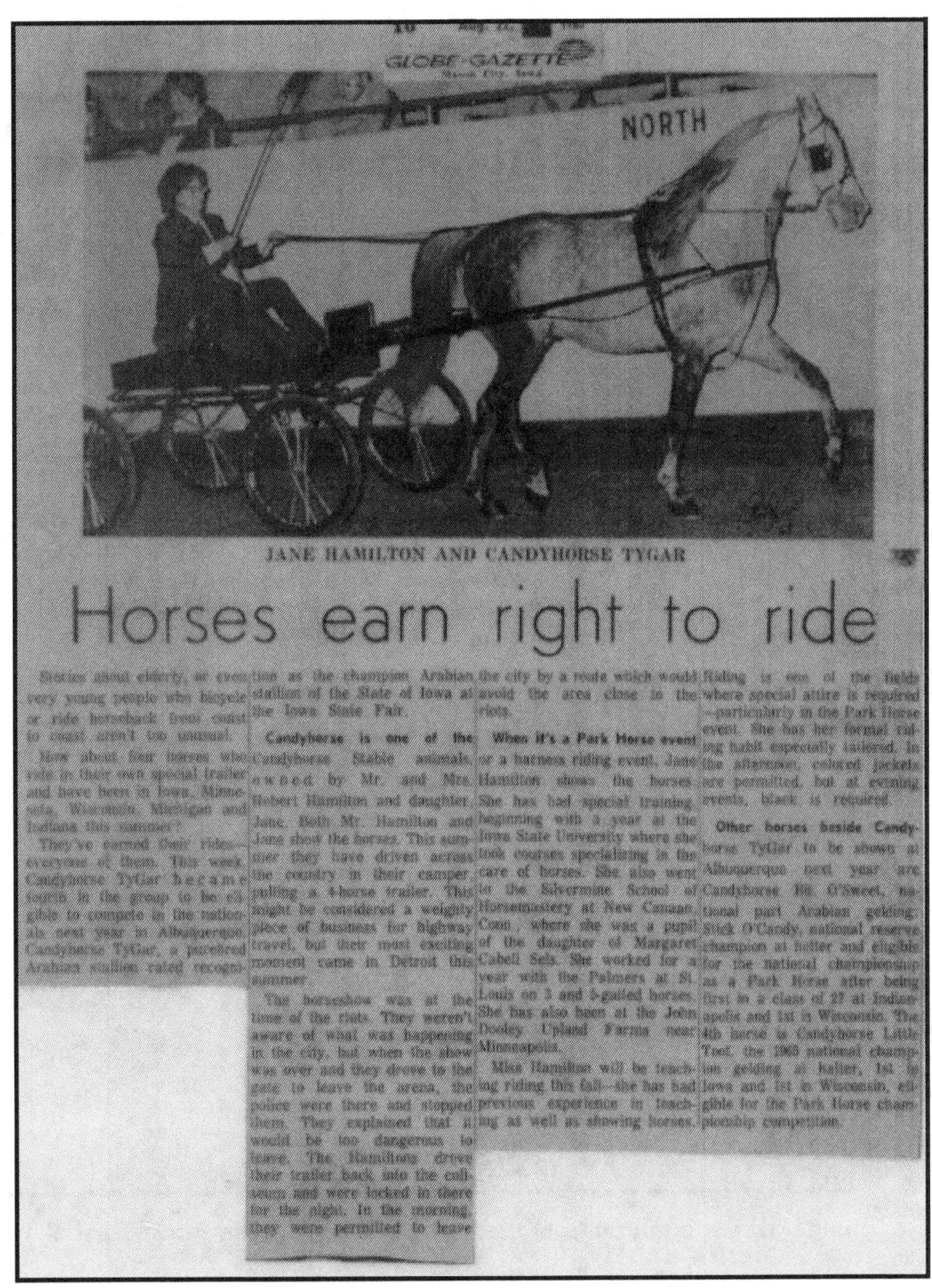

JANE HAMILTON AND CANDYHORSE TYGAR

Horses earn right to ride

Stories about elderly, or even very young people who bicycle or ride horseback from coast to coast aren't too unusual.

How about four horses who ride in their own special trailer and have been in Iowa, Minnesota, Wisconsin, Michigan and Indiana this summer?

They've earned their rides, everyone of them. This week Candyhorse Tygar became fourth in the group to be eligible to compete in the nationals next year in Albuquerque. Candyhorse Tygar, a purebred Arabian stallion rated recognition as the champion Arabian stallion of the State of Iowa at the Iowa State Fair.

Candyhorse is one of the Candyhorse Stable animals owned by Mr. and Mrs. Robert Hamilton and daughter, Jane. Both Mr. Hamilton and Jane show the horses. This summer they have driven across the country in their camper pulling a 4-horse trailer. This might be considered a weighty piece of business for highway travel, but their most exciting moment came in Detroit this summer.

The horseshow was at the time of the riots. They weren't aware of what was happening in the city, but when the show was over and they drove to the gate to leave the arena, the police were there and stopped them. They explained that it would be too dangerous to leave. The Hamiltons drove their trailer back into the coliseum and were locked in there for the night. In the morning they were permitted to leave the city by a route which would avoid the area close to the riots.

When it's a Park Horse event or a harness riding event, Jane Hamilton shows the horses. She has had special training beginning with a year at the Iowa State University where she took courses specializing in the care of horses. She also went to the Silvermine School of Horsemastery at New Canaan, Conn., where she was a pupil of the daughter of Margaret Cabell Self. She worked for a year with the Palmers at St. Louis on 3 and 5-gaited horses. She has also been at the John Dooley Upland Farms near Minneapolis.

Miss Hamilton will be teaching riding this fall—she has had previous experience in teaching as well as showing horses.

Riding is one of the fields where special attire is required—particularly in the Park Horse event. She has her formal riding habit especially tailored. In the afternoon, colored jackets are permitted, but at evening events, black is required.

Other horses beside Candy-horse Tygar to be shown at Albuquerque next year are Candyhorse Big O'Sweet, national part Arabian gelding; Stick O'Candy, national reserve champion at halter and eligible for the national championship as a Park Horse after being first in a class of 27 at Indianapolis and 1st in Wisconsin. The 4th horse is Candyhorse Little Toot, the 1963 national champion gelding at halter, 1st in Iowa and 1st in Wisconsin, eligible for the Park Horse championship competition.

Another newspaper article featuring the accomplishments of the Candyhorse Farm and it's Arabians.

INTERNATIONAL ARABIAN HORSE ASSOCIATION

P.O. Box 33696, Denver, Colorado 80233-0696   303-450-4774

August 14, 1986

Ms. Jane Marie Hamilton
Post Office Box 1086
Norman OK 73070

Dear Ms. Hamilton:

This year marks the 20th anniversary of the U. S. NATIONAL ARABIAN AND
HALF-ARABIAN CHAMPIONSHIP HORSE SHOW. In commemoration of this event, the
International Arabian Horse Association plans to recognize all of the past
U. S. National Champions in a very special way.

As the one-time owner of the following National Champion(s):

                    CANDYHORSE LITTLE TOOT

we request your assistance in providing an 8" x 10" color photograph of the
horse(s). We would appreciate receiving the picture by August 26, 1986 in
order to be included in IAHA's special tribute. If you would like your
photograph(s) returned, please so indicate.

There are a number of older National Champion horses whose owners are no
longer on any of our mailing lists. If you have access to photographs of
National Champions other than those listed above and are willing to share
them, please submit with the other(s).

Thank you for your help and your participation in this very special event.

Sincerely,

Paulette A. Schroeder
Special Projects Administrator

PAS/s

Letter of Recognition from the International Arabian Horse Association.

Tyzara (Candyhorse Ty Gar x Zarife"s Sahara) owned by Roseann Suddarth of Moore, Oklahoma

Palomar Playmate, sired by Candyhorse Ty Gar and his dam American Moonbaby.

Candyhorse The Lady Leonie (Candyhorse Ty Gar x Candyhorse Mamzal) owned by the Jackson family in Oklahoma, became a National Top Ten Trail horse

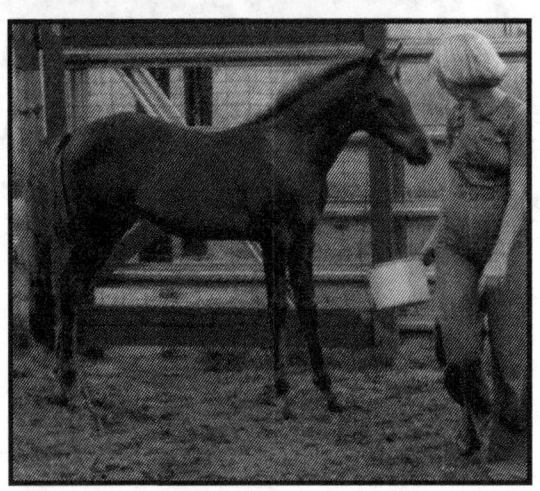

Mariah's Whisper and Susan Bennett of McCloud, Oklahoma

Candyhorse Ty Gar's Tucson (Candyhorse Ty Gar x Candyhorse Mamzal)

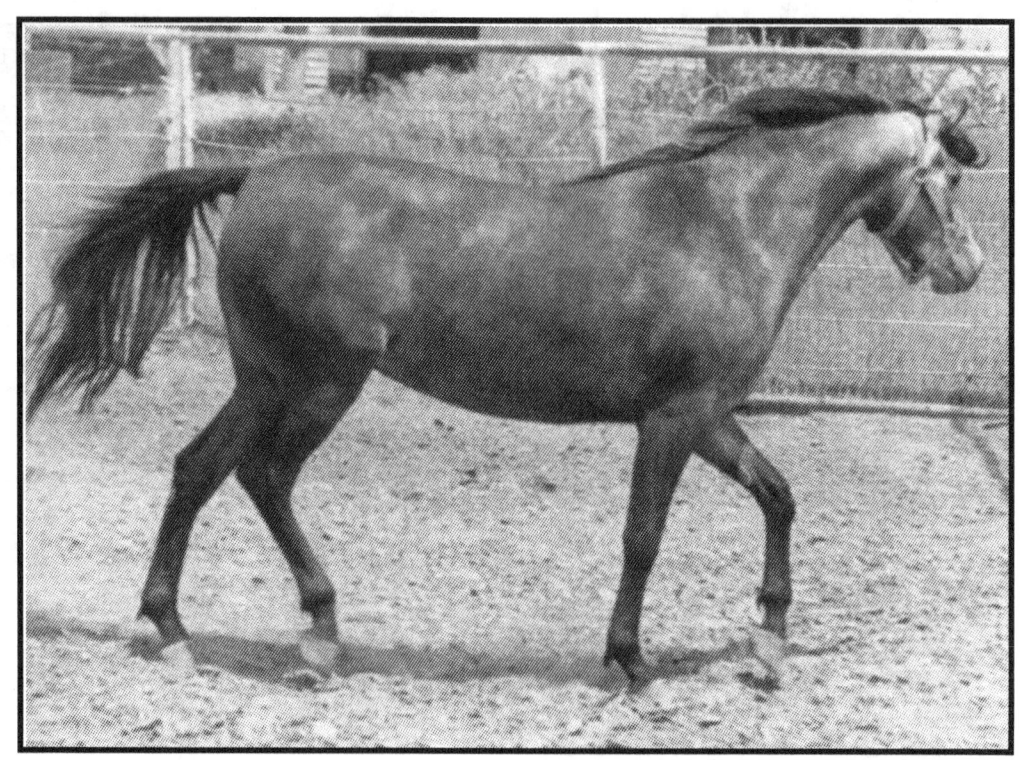

Candyhorse Tattyput (Candyhorse Ty Gar x Bay Lady Love)

Verindty (Candyhorse Ty Gar x Ambrosia's Verity) and Mr. Bill Suddarth, a retired firechief of Chickasha, Oklahoma

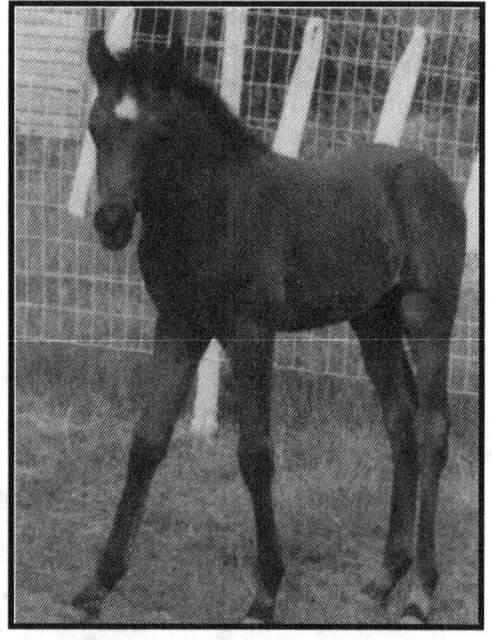

Candyhorse Ty Gar's Kitten (Candyhorse Ty Gar x Bay Lady Love)

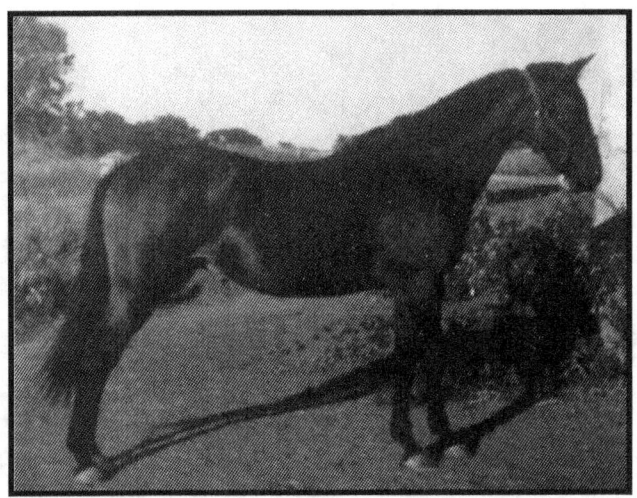

Bay Lady Love (Mi Mary's King Girl)

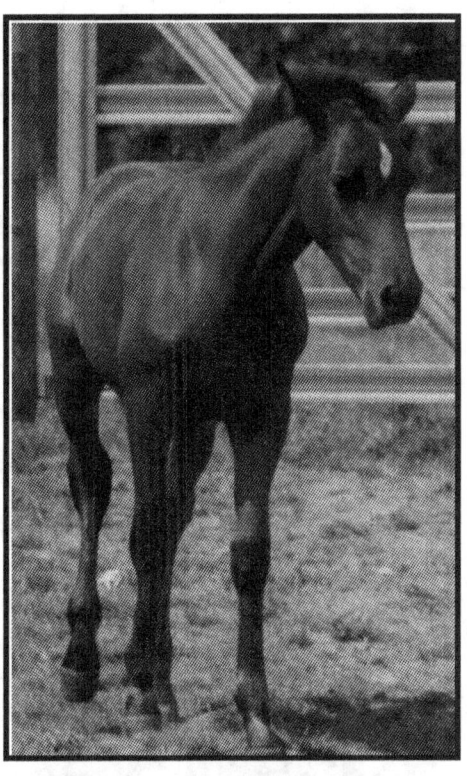

**Mariah's Chickadee
(Candyhorse Ty Gar x Neci)**

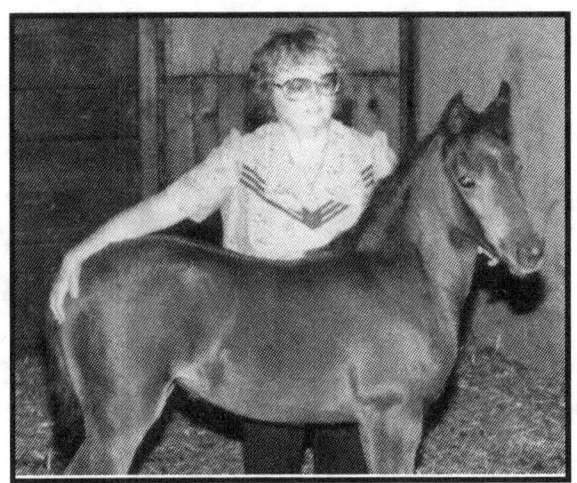

Ty Gar's Tattyput and Honey.

**Dandee Dawn (Candyhorse Ty Gar
x SynaBrosia) owned by the
Sackett family of Denton, Texas**

**Mariah's Whisper (Candyhorse Ty
Gar x American Moonbaby) with
her family in Oklahoma.**

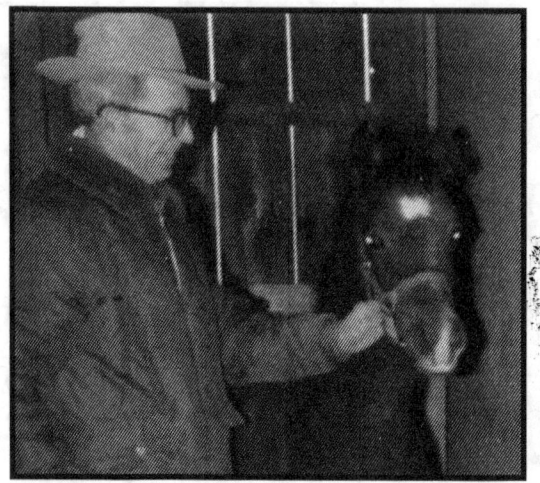

Joe Butterfly and Mister (Bob Hamilton)

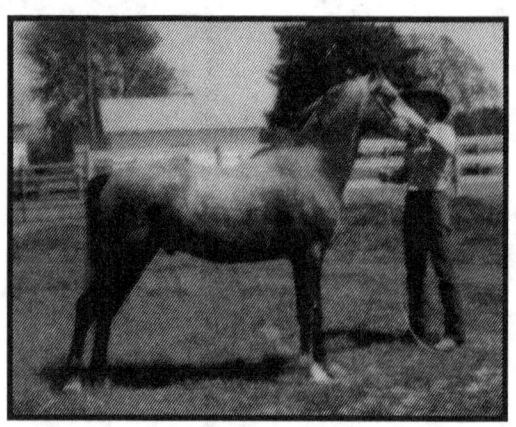

Joe Butterfly (Candyhorse Ty Gar x SynaBrosia) and Red Byers

Red Byers, legendary horse trainer in Joplin, Missouri, said Joe Butterfly was the last pleasure horse he would train and that he trained him for himself.

The current Candyhorse Farm located on Highway 90 in Grand Ridge, Fl.

Tazzraf Matar (Prince Tazzraf x Bint Abril) The Candyhorse Farm's present senior stallion.

Blizzara (Jon-San Blizzard x Golden Glo Zaroufa)

Precendence PR (Standing Ovation x *Porsza

Purr Butterfly (Joe Butterfly x Diamond's Charm)

Sarhita (Siegmund x Segan)

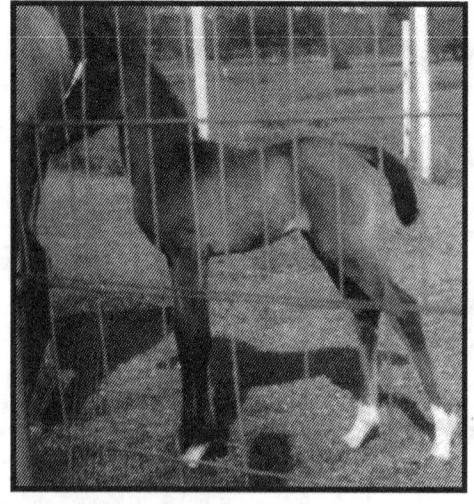

Prencessh (Shadimar x Precedence PR)

Bob and Jane Hamilton with Les Boomhower, founder of the Pony of the Americas breed.

www.ingramcontent.com/pod-product-compliance
Lightning Source LLC
Chambersburg PA
CBHW080414290526
45791CB00008BA/2266